Clodagh Dunlop

A Return to Duty

The remarkable story of how a young woman
fought her way out of locked-in syndrome, and
recovered, against all the odds.

Acknowledgements

I would like to acknowledge and express my gratitude to every person who has come into my life following my brainstem stroke on 6 April 2015.

The wonderful human beings that make up our NHS saved my life and without them I would never have had my journey of recovery. Angels are nurses working in our hospitals.

To Sue Leonard, who listened to me and was invaluable in helping me with this book and putting my words on paper. For her editing, Alicia McAuley.

All my friends, for their love and support. KD, Fiona and Ruth who were always by my side through my journey.

My amazing family whose love and support knows no limits: Dave and Mags, your unfailing love blows me away. Adrian and Diane, I feel every breath I take is because you believed in me and the courage you had every day.

Published 2019 by Clodagh Dunlop
©2019 Clodagh Dunlop
All rights reserved
ISBN 978-1-5272-5198-4

Designed by April Sky Design & Colourpoint Creative Limited, Newtownards
www.aprilsky.co.uk

About the Author

Clodagh Dunlop is a detective in the Police Service of Northern Ireland. Her life was turned upside down in April 2015 when she suffered a brainstem stroke, which left her with locked-in syndrome. There is no cure for locked-in syndrome and she was expected to be a prisoner in her own body forever. However, Clodagh astonished her doctors, family and colleagues with her determination and courage when faced with the life-changing condition. Although she still has some disabilities, Clodagh has recovered sufficiently to return to work full time, carrying out all the duties that her role as a detective entails.

Clodagh has documented her recovery on social media, gaining a supportive following across the world. She has won numerous awards for her inspirational recovery, including Belfast Telegraph Woman of the Year, British Association for Women in Policing Inspirational Officer and the Stroke Association Adult Courage Award. As well as working full time, Clodagh provides motivational lectures to business and health professionals. As a respected and recognisable advocate for stroke survivors, Clodagh has lobbied government ministers in Westminster for legislation to reshape stroke services.

CHAPTER ONE

Waking to a Nightmare

I open my eyes. I'm alive. But where am I? There are flashing lights, the beeping and swishing noises of machines. It feels like a sci-fi movie. Am I in a spaceship? Am I in a parallel dimension? Am I hallucinating? Blinking, I focus my eyes and concentrate, taking in all I can see. I realise I am in hospital. There are wires coming from both my arms; there are tubes in my mouth and another up my nose. For a brief moment, I think, *Yes, I was right! I* am *ill – and they didn't listen to me.*

I hope the nurse feels really bad – the one in A & E who shouted and accused me of being on drugs. I imagine confronting her and saying, 'I *told* you I was ill.'

But my satisfaction quickly changes to anger. I realise I'm in pain. And it's a kind of pain I've never felt before.

I try to move my head to look around. Nothing happens. I try moving my arms, my legs; I try shifting my body in the bed. The white sheet that is covering me doesn't move. Nothing moves. I panic and scream, but I hear nothing – only the beeping machines. I haven't made a sound. A figure walks past my bed and I follow it with my eyes. I follow until my eyeballs hurt with the strain. Every part of my body is in agony. What is happening to me? My brain is racing. How did all this start? And then, slowly, it comes back to me.

Easter Monday ... alone at home ... a feeling of death ... my sister, Diane ... the hospital ... hands on me, voices ... nobody believes I'm unwell ... a nurse shouts, 'What drugs have you taken, Clodagh?'

And that's the last thing I remember.

But this isn't A & E. It's too quiet. Is it intensive care? If I'm in intensive care, that means I'm seriously ill. Why did nobody believe me?

A nurse appears and looks at me intently. She has brown hair and a kind face. Noticing that my eyes are open, she says, 'Clodagh, you're awake.' My eyes follow her as she moves around my bed. She examines the beeping monitors and gently adjusts some tubes beside my bed. As she does this, I realise that I have the other end of one tube in my mouth. It hurts. It is pressing my tongue onto my teeth. That must mean I can't breathe by myself. Both my arms have wires coming from them. And is that a second tube going up into my nose? I realise that machines must be keeping me alive. I've never been so scared.

Looking down at me, the nurse asks, 'Can you hear me?'

I want to say yes – but how can I with these tubes in my mouth? A sense of terror is building. I'm fully alert now and I realise that every part of my body is in unbearable pain. It's worst in my mouth. It feels like the teeth in my lower jaw are going to cut through my tongue. What is happening to me?

'Clodagh?' She has raised her voice. 'Can you hear me?'

Yes, yes, yes!

Shaking her head, she lets out a sigh. I've made no sound. I keep trying to move my arms, my mouth and tongue. I stare at her, willing her to read my eyes. I try to glare at her, to smile at her. Nothing happens. Her facial expression doesn't change. How can I let her know that I can hear her? How can I let her know that I've never been in this much pain? That I need someone to move my tongue to stop the tube pressing on it? She then speaks to me very slowly, loudly and deliberately.

'Clodagh, you are in the Royal Victoria Hospital in Belfast, and you have had a stroke.'

The word rings in my ears. A stroke? I've had a stroke? Surely not! Strokes only happen to old people, don't they? Not fit, healthy, 35-year-old police officers like me. That can't be right! The Royal Victoria Hospital? In Belfast? But the ambulance took me to a different hospital. How have I got here?

I think about what I know about strokes. Surely one side of my body should be fine? But I can't move anything. Not even a fingertip. Maybe they have given me the wrong medication and completely paralysed me! How do I let them know? If only this tube wasn't in my mouth – then I'd be able to talk. But what if they kill me before the tube in my mouth is taken out? This cannot be happening to me. It must be some horrible nightmare.

Then fresh pain shoots through every part of me and I stop thinking altogether.

The kind-faced nurse comes back, peers at me and says, 'Clodagh, how do you feel?'

I stare into her face and will her with everything I can muster to read in my eyes: *I am in the most awful pain.* But she doesn't react. I keep staring at her face into her eyes. I'm screaming at her in my head. *Please!* But I can't make a sound. She doesn't realise I'm here. The tubes are getting heavier in my mouth, pressing my tongue harder against my teeth. I try to free my tongue but nothing happens. I can't understand it. It's as if my body has been disconnected from my brain.

Why can't I move my head? I stare at the fibreglass ceiling tiles above me. They look like they've been spattered with pepper. I notice every detail in each tile. I have to let someone know I'm here and I've been given the wrong medication. I think about this and decide to try again. I will my legs, then my arms, then my fingers to move. Then, my body does move, but it doesn't follow my instructions. Instead it jerks violently and every muscle in my body feels like it's going to tear. How can no one realise I'm in horrendous pain? I'm in intensive care! In my head I scream again. I wait for a nurse to come running, but nobody comes.

Pain is ripping through every muscle in my body, from the soles of my feet to the top of my head. It feels like someone has put forks into all my muscles and is pulling each of them in opposite directions, shredding each muscle like a piece of beef.

This is Diane's fault. I did die – I'm sure of it – and she brought me back. I can't bear this pain. It is torture. I want to die.

Then, at last, the kind-faced nurse notices.

'Do you think she is having more seizures?'

The nurse is frowning, but she isn't talking to me. Nobody is. Why doesn't anyone realise I'm here? People in white coats and blue tunics busy themselves around me, talking about scans and tests as they check the beeping monitors. Do machines monitor pain? Why don't they talk to *me*? Is there any way, without being able to make a sound, that I can tell them how bad it is, that this pain is killing me?

I'm here! Look at me!

'Clodagh, we're taking you for a CT scan.'

The nurse's eyes don't rest on mine.

I hear a clunk and my bed starts to move. The wheels on my bed make a rumbling sound as they turn. I stare at the white ceiling tiles above me as we travel the long hospital corridors. If I could move my head I might be able to let people know I'm here. Air rushes over my face and arms. It feels wonderful – a relief after the hot, sterile atmosphere in intensive care. Doors shut in the distance and I hear chatter and laughter. Bits of conversation drift over me as we glide along. There are people in hospital uniforms walking alongside me, but for all the notice they take of me I might as well be alone. Alone with God, perhaps. I'm not religious. I don't rush to church, but God does exist for me. And now, it's just him and me – and *he* isn't listening.

I keep shouting and arguing with him, because I have nobody else. Nobody at all.

How is it possible to be alive and in a hospital, yet experiencing this level of pain? How can I not be dead?

I plead with him: *Let me die!* But nothing happens. I beg him: *Please, please, let me go! I want to die.* But he doesn't answer. Is he even there?

We whoosh through double doors and my bed comes to a stop. I see a man in a smart suit, sitting down. I instantly recognise him as a member of our local political assembly. He turns from a conversation and, catching sight of me, seems overcome with sadness. I stare at him. Surely *he* will realise I'm here. He shakes his head slightly, pity etched on his face. I must really look ill. I must really *be* ill! This can't be happening!

I play back that look inside my head as I'm manoeuvred from my hospital bed onto a table for the CT scan. At the end of the table is a weird industrial-looking doughnut. Voices chatter over me. The table moves me inside the doughnut. Then silence. I'm alone. The doughnut begins to make a whirring sound. It feels like I'm in a washing machine. This whole thing is just bizarre. Everyone can see my motionless body but no one realises I'm here. I can't move. I can't speak. Is it possible that this is real? This only happens to people on television or in the movies. But me? I'm just an ordinary woman.

When the scan is finished I'm wheeled back down the long corridors. I can tell when we move to different parts of the hospital by changes in the ceiling. I can't see the faces belonging to the voices I hear. Trying to see the faces hurts my eyes. I am attempting to turn my eyeballs further than they will go. All I want is for one of them to talk to me!

I know we are back in intensive care when my bed comes to a sudden stop and I hear a clunk. It is darker here than in the corridors. Intensive care must have no windows.

I feel relief when I hear a familiar voice.

'Is she having more seizures?' The kind-faced nurse stares at me. All I want is to somehow let her know I'm here. Then a new face stares at me and a series of hands pull me around, trying to sit me up. No chance of that, I think, as I slump back into the bed like a puppet whose strings have been cut. The new face peels the backing off an electrode and places it on the side of my forehead. I feel her press firmly on the electrode for a few seconds. She repeats the process at least ten times until there are electrodes all over my head. She stands back and stares at me. Her face looks like my mum's when she is decorating the Christmas tree, checking how she's arranged the baubles.

I fill up with anticipation. *Good*, I think. *Maybe the new face will work it out – I'm here and I'm in unbearable pain.*

'She's *not* having seizures,' the new face pronounces. Tension leaks from the room. The new face can't see me after all. I want to scream at them all: *You're medically trained! Every single one of you! But you can't see the distress I'm in? Look at me! How can you not know? Why can't you work it out?*

The kind-faced nurse tweaks at a cannula in my hand. It nips my skin. She hovers beside my bed. I feel liquid flush into my hand through the cannula. Almost immediately, in spite of the pain and anger, I fall asleep.

I don't know how much time has passed when I awake. I hear the sound of crying. There are figures at the end of my bed. I pick out my parents. They look older, somehow, than they did when I saw them last. My dad's face is a terrible shade of grey. Diane is there, and there's a tall woman with them, her hands over her face, sobbing. I recognise my best friend, KD, and wonder what she's doing here. She's distraught. Am I dying? Are they all here to say goodbye to me?

I don't need their tears – I need their help. But it's hopeless. I concentrate. If I focus, like in meditation, I will make my muscles relax and the pain will lessen. Shutting my eyes to block them all out, I fall asleep again.

A voice disturbs my sleep.

'Clodagh, you are in the Royal Victoria Hospital, Belfast. You have had a stroke.'

It is the kind-faced nurse, using the same words.

That word – 'stroke'.

Yes, I know, I say in my head. *I heard you before! Will you* please *get me something for the pain?*

I hear her say to someone, 'I think I'll wash her hair. It's dirty.'

Dirty? My hair? It can't be. I'm obsessed with cleanliness. I shower every day without fail, often twice a day. How could my hair be dirty? I'm still indignant when my head is lifted up by gentle hands. Then I feel warm water run over my head and the gentle massage of fingers on my scalp. The unbearable pain in my muscles has subsided. I feel a dull ache all over my body. The nurse talks to me, reassuringly, as if she knows I can hear. Does she realise I actually can? I like my kind-faced nurse.

Maybe it's whatever they put in the cannula, but I start to feel peaceful. The pain is leaving my body; the fog in my brain is dissolving. I remember. I know why my hair is so dirty. I remember how I vomited in A & E, and how the vomit covered not just my hair, but my clothes and the floor as well, as my body writhed across the bed, as if it had been taken over by aliens.

CHAPTER TWO

Clodagh, Are You There?

I wake up. It's a new day. I have survived the night and the pain has gone. I'm relieved. Maybe it was all a bad dream. But I lift my hand to scratch an itch on my nose and nothing happens. I still can't move. My body is a dead weight.

This nightmare is real.

A new nurse approaches me. She's smiling.

'Well! You look brighter this morning,' she says cheerily, whooshing the curtains around me. 'It's time to get you ready for the day, Clodagh.' How is she going to get my useless body ready? And for what?

Pulling back the sheet, she undresses me. I feel shocked. The nurse is behaving like this is the most natural thing in the world, but I'm horrified. I am lying, naked, in front of a complete stranger. I feel cool air move over my body as a fan blows at the end of my bed. Somehow the breeze makes me more conscious of my nakedness. She gets a basin of warm water and gently washes my body. I feel a tug between my legs. I suddenly realise I have a catheter. I haven't thought about what happens when I need the bathroom. What happens when my bowels move? As the nurse rolls me unto my side, she places what I can only assume is an adult nappy under my bottom.

I want to cry.

I'm as helpless as a newborn baby. More helpless, in fact. At least a baby can breathe. I have a machine doing that for me. A baby can feed, make noise, kick its legs and wave its arms around. I can't even move a fingertip.

The kind-faced nurse said when I first woke that I'd had a stroke; but that must be a mistake. If I had, surely I'd be able to move a little? I think of the doctors and the way they worked around me as if I wasn't even there. And then it dawns on me. They think I'm brain dead!

I'm stuck in this bed, completely and utterly helpless. There is nothing I can do to change that. I have no control over anything – and I never will, unless someone works out *I'm here*!

6

This can't be me. This can't be my new reality. I feel utter terror.

Clodagh, nothing scares you. It will be okay, I tell myself. It's true – I wasn't scared of anything – but that was when I could move and talk. Now I am completely helpless and I have never felt this terrified. What if no one realises I'm still conscious? Will they turn off the machines?

My thoughts come to a sudden halt when Adrian's face peers into mine. I'm relieved to see him, but surprised. How did he get here? The last I knew he was in Scotland. He's wearing a freshly ironed shirt and he looks handsome with his bearded face. I smile inside but the happiness soon evaporates. I become frantic. What if *he* thinks I'm brain dead? Of all people, I need him to realise I'm still here. But how can I do that?

Looking serious, he leans over and kisses me carefully on my forehead, avoiding all the tubes. I want him to put his arms around me and to hold me tight. I want to tell him all about the nightmare that has been happening to me since I visited him in Scotland. His eyes are bloodshot. He must have had to rush home when someone told him I was in hospital. Who told him? Was he as shocked as me that I've had a stroke?

I stare into his eyes and he stares back at me. There are so many things I want to say to him, but I can't. I feel like an astronaut, detached from my spacecraft and drifting off into space. I'm screaming for help, bursting with emotion, yet no one can hear my million thoughts.

Why can't I make a noise? He keeps staring into my eyes, as if searching for clues. I hold my stare back at him.

Please, Adrian! I need you to realise I'm still here.

'Hello, pet,' he says.

Hello, pet? I want to scream. *Is that all you can say? You can't be serious, Adrian!*

I hope he can read the anger in my eyes because right now I'm saying, *I* hate *you, Adrian!*

Then a miracle happens.

'Clodagh, are you there?' he asks, still staring into my eyes.

I look at him. I stare as hard as I can into his eyes.

Yes, yes, yes! I love you!

'*Please* tell me you're there, Clodagh!'

This is the most important moment of my entire life. I *must* let him know that I can understand him. He *has* to know I am still his Clodagh, his running partner, the only person who can beat him at chess. But how can I do that? My mouth won't move; nothing moves. I'm being held prisoner by my own body.

Adrian will make this nightmare end; but he has to know that I can still think and feel. He knows me better than anyone else. The doctors and nurses have never met me. If he doesn't see me, how can they be expected to?

I stare into his eyes, holding his gaze, praying harder than I ever have.

Please, Adrian. See life in me.

His expression doesn't change. My heart sinks. Then a second miracle happens. He finds a way for me to tell him.

'Clodagh, if you *are* there … if you can hear me … blink. Blink once. Can you do that?'

Can I? I have no idea. My eyelids have been opening and closing, it's true, but do I have any control over them? I don't know. What if I can't make myself blink? What if I just manage to flutter my eyelids? If I do – or if I give two or three blinks by mistake – he won't get the message. He will think I'm brain dead, like the rest of them. I can't get this wrong. Please, God, let my eyelids work.

If I'm going to survive, I *must* get this right.

I shut my eyes slowly, tightly, concentrating with every ounce of energy. I wait. I count slowly – one, two, three. Then, very deliberately, I open my eyes as wide as I can and look steadily up at Adrian. I search his face anxiously.

He smiles at me. *Yes! I did it. He knows I'm here!* If I could, I'd spring out of bed and hug him. He might just have saved my life.

Thank God!

'Thank God!'

I can hear the relief in his voice. The worry clears from his face. Still smiling, he looks at me and puts his hand on my hand, trying to avoid all the wires coming from it. 'I knew it,' he says. 'Deep down I knew it. You are just too fit for a stroke to beat you. You've been training all this time to fight for your life. You're strong – and you're stubborn!'

I am so happy I could burst! He knows the fighting-fit police officer inside this paralysed body. He holds my gaze.

'Clodagh, listen to me. You will be okay. I promise you. We are going to get through this together.' He says it with such certainty and such incredible positivity I believe him. There isn't a part of me that doubts him. Looking into his eyes, I feel so relieved. Now Adrian knows I'm here, I *will* be okay.

Adrian sits down on a chair beside my bed. I'm annoyed. Does he not realise I can't move my head? It doesn't matter. I love him so much right now. I turn my eyes as far as they will go so I can see him. The chair is next to the beeping machines keeping me alive. I find the presence of Adrian and the repetitive beeps reassuring. I think about medical dramas on television. It's a change in the beeps that means something is wrong. Constant short beeps are good.

Looking at me, Adrian begins to talk. He tells me how shocked he was when he was first told that this terrible thing had happened to me. I try and let him know with my eyes: *I know what you mean. I'm in shock too.* I want him to tell me why it has happened and when I can go home to the house we bought together.

I remember when it was just a half-finished building on my regular running route, set down beneath the road, that I dreamed of buying. My dad told me I needed two things from a house. Firstly, it should be a bungalow I could grow old in; second, I should be able to walk to the shop from it to buy a newspaper and a jar of milk. This one was a bungalow and within walking distance of a newsagent's. We did manage to buy it in the end, and when we moved in we put a sandstone plaque on the gate, naming it the 'Forever House'.

I hate intensive care. I want so much for him to pick me up and take me home.

He tells me how difficult it was to park at the hospital – but, because I'm in intensive care, the parking is free. He laughs at that and in my head so do I. I know he has told me this because he knows I would chastise him and laugh. I feel like we're having a conversation; and that he can understand me, even though I'm moving only my eyelids. I feel safe listening to the sound of Adrian's voice.

My peace ends abruptly when a sudden stabbing pain in my tongue reminds me of the nightmare world I've entered. My mouth is in agony. I realise that I'm now angry with Adrian. If he understands me as I feel he does, why can't he tell that my mouth is so sore? Can't he see that the tubes are pressing my tongue onto my teeth? Isn't it obvious? Can't he see that my mouth is dry and I desperately need water? Now he knows I'm here, why doesn't he get out his mobile phone and work out a way for us to have a conversation? I'm not exactly sure how, but shouldn't he be trying, at least?

He tells me about his journey home from Scotland. He says it was two days ago, and I try and work out how long I was unconscious for. I take in every word he tells me to try and understand what has happened. He is filling in the pieces of the puzzle that I am missing. But he's not giving me all the detail I need. I have so many questions. This is frustrating.

'And the next thing I went into this room and there you were, lying on life support, with tubes coming out of everywhere and your eyelids taped down. They'd put you in a coma. You looked dead to the world. It was terrifying – like seeing a body laid out for a post mortem.'

Post mortems are normal for us. We've both attended lots of them as police officers. Still, I just can't picture myself laid out like a corpse on a mortuary table. 'This isn't real, I thought. This can't be the happy, smiley Clodagh with the pony tail I waved off in Glasgow Airport.'

The doctor told Adrian I was being transferred to Belfast and asked him if he'd like to escort the trolley down to the ambulance. They told him to say goodbye to me in case I didn't survive the journey.

'That's when it actually hit me,' he says. 'You might die.' He pauses. 'It just didn't feel real. Walking down the corridors of a hospital, looking at you, I couldn't believe what I was seeing. They lifted you into the ambulance and I could see all these machines, and a crowd of doctors and nurses going with you to try and keep you alive. Then the door closed and off you went. And there I was, standing there in complete shock, thinking, *How the hell has this happened to Clodagh?*'

It's strange to think of myself in the back of an ambulance, the one needing help. On duty I was frequently in ambulances at the scene of road-traffic collisions. But I was the one giving help, reassuring people I'd helped into the ambulance. And now I find out I was being rushed to the Royal Victoria Hospital, sirens blaring, blue lights flashing and a whole team of medics keeping me alive. My partner not knowing if I'd make the journey.

'You know, the doctors really thought you might die. Right there, in the ambulance.'

But I didn't. I survived the journey. I had surgery, Adrian tells me – a procedure to remove the clot from the base of my brain. They got it out by threading a wire through my groin to the base of my brain. And, somehow, I was still alive at the end of that horrific day.

When Adrian gets up to leave, I notice he is wearing my thumb ring. So *that's* where it went! I noticed my jewellery had disappeared – some of the things that make me *me* – and I'd been upset. Someone had taken my clothes, too. I am wearing a hideous cream nightdress with lace on it – something an old woman would wear. Has my mum brought a nightdress from my grandmother's house? Where has it come from? Why hasn't she brought my pyjamas? I'm a pyjama woman. She knows that.

As Adrian disappears from my view, I close my eyes in despair.

I met Adrian at work, but I didn't like him at first. He was Sergeant Simpson to me. He was strict, serious and correct, and he always had to be right. I avoided him whenever I could and made a point of leaving my paperwork in his office when he wasn't there.

The irony, I think. I didn't even like this man two years ago – and now I don't want him to leave my bedside. We suit each other because in many ways we are alike. In many ways, he is the male version of me. I am serious. I always have to be right. I like adventure and I like to travel outside of work. He does too.

Last year we took off for southern Africa, living out of a tent for six weeks. Starting in Cape Town, we travelled the west coast to Namibia, before crossing into Botswana, taking in Zambia and Zimbabwe before finishing in Johannesburg. It was magical. Seeing the dramatic landscapes along with the wildlife – elephants, giraffes and zebras – made me fall in love with the continent of Africa. I feel like I want to explore more of it. And living every day with Adrian in our tent made me realise how much I liked him being part of my life.

Adrian took up running when we started dating. I was sure he did this only to impress me – he knew how much I loved putting on my trainers and running for miles. I was always faster than him; I made sure of it. He said that was because he was five years older than me, but I would tell him it was because I was simply a better runner than him.

When we had a night off, we would run together, then sit in the hot tub I had bought on Gumtree. We would open a bottle of wine, sit under the night sky for hours and talk about life. We would go inside when our skin was wrinkled, put on what we called 'dance me' music and dance. Our 'dance me' music was a playlist of songs that reminded me of different countries I've travelled to. It wasn't music from those countries, just bands like Coldplay, Green Day and U2. I associated those songs with happy times and Adrian liked them too. Nobody was watching; we could be as silly and crazy as we wanted.

One of those nights, sitting in the hot tub, I told Adrian I knew that something bad was going to happen to me. Something was going to go wrong. He said I was being silly. It was hard to explain to him because I didn't understand it myself. I didn't know if it was police-officer gut instinct or female intuition, but I knew there was something in my future that was going to challenge me to my core. I was sure of it.

I feel angry with myself. I should have trusted my instinct. I should have been more persistent with the doctors in hospital. I'm still thinking about this when I hear the rustling of a bag and feel the weight of an object pressed against my legs. I open my eyes. Diane is smiling down at me.

'Well, drama queen! Adrian says you can understand us. Can you?'

I am so happy he has told Diane. I blink repeatedly.

'So, I've collected pyjamas from your house and I got you some new creams.' Diane unscrews the lid from a small pink tub and shoves it under my nose. 'Smell that – it's lovely. Look at your lips. They're awfully dry and cracked. Are they sore?'

When Diane is very chatty, like this, I know she is nervous. Right now I love her nervous chatter.

'I'm going to see is there something for your lips.' She disappears, then appears just as quickly, looking proud of herself. 'I got this.' Diane waves a tiny little stick with a small sponge attached. 'And I got you a bottle of fresh water from the fridge, but I'm not allowed to really use it. I had to promise I'd squeeze the water out of the sponge and not have it too wet because I might choke you! Will I rub it on your lips?'

I blink repeatedly. Diane places the small sponge on my lips. 'Is that okay?'

'Diane, be careful! Don't kill her!' It's Mum.

I want to tell Diane to ignore Mum – this is brilliant. Who knew a little tiny sponge on a stick would help ease my torture? I blink frantically.

'See? She likes it. I won't kill her. Why don't you rub cream on her legs?'

'Would I be allowed?' Mum sounds more nervous than Diane.

'Yes – it's your daughter. Stop being silly. Clodagh, do you want her to rub cream on your legs?'

I blink frantically.

'See? She wants you to.'

I wish I could tell Diane I love her. I love her smile. No one smiles in intensive care. I love the way she is so busy – her energy makes me feel alive. I love the way she is acting like there is nothing wrong with me worse than a bad dose of flu. But I know her. I'm the strong, adrenaline-loving sister. I love exploring the world. Diane is softer, gentle, thoughtful, a homebird. She's in denial that this is serious.

'Mummy, not like that. Here, let me.'

Diane takes over massaging my legs. It feels amazing. She doesn't stop talking for a full hour. She keeps sponging my lips, then goes back to massaging my legs. She chatters about her kids, Emily, Adam and Hannah. I blink frantically when she pauses, just to let her know I'm listening. She tells Mum to tidy my bedside locker.

Good idea, Diane, I want to say, *keeping Mum busy.*

'We will see you tomorrow.' Diane gently kisses my forehead. 'I love you. You will beat this.'

My heart lurches. I don't want them to go. I want Mum and Diane to stay. I love them. I want Adrian to come back. I don't want to be here alone. They talk to me. Being alone with your own thoughts when you don't know what is happening to you is a living hell.

Don't go, Diane! Take me home! Please!

I stare into her eyes, pleading, willing her to read my thoughts.

I don't understand what is happening to me. I need you, Diane!

My eyes fill with tears. I can't see Diane, but I can hear her.

'Please Clodagh, don't. You're going to be okay. I promise.'

Diane is sobbing. I can hear Mum sobbing too.

'Please. We will be back. Adrian is coming later. There won't be a day we all won't be here. We love you. I know you are going to get better.' I feel Diane kiss my forehead again.

The tears are stinging my eyes. I can't watch them leave. I hear Diane's voice fade into the distance. They have gone.

I feel alone. No one will think to wipe my eyes, despite how they are hurting me. The awful pain has gone now, but I'm uncomfortable all the time. The nappy under my bum is always annoying me, and there are other things driving me mad – a wisp of hair across my face that I can't sweep away, a sheet covering my feet when I want them out in the air, my nightdress being crumpled beneath my body. I know I'll be here in this position for hours, with no one who will talk to me. I fill with despair.

But Adrian knows I'm here. He knows I'm not brain dead. He will sort this out. I cling to that thought, telling myself that I'll be home soon, talking to Adrian about this in the hot tub some night. Now he knows I'm here, he will bring me home.

CHAPTER THREE

Time Slows Down

I stare at the ceiling tiles as I wait for visiting time. I imagine that the spattered pepper marks on the ceiling tiles are stars and try to make the Big Dipper. Adrian and I slept under the stars in Africa. We tried to find constellations. I close my eyes as tight as I can and try to remember every detail of the African night sky. It was breathtakingly beautiful. The cicadas were singing. I never knew an insect could be so loud.

I open my eyes. I sense someone beside me. My father is staring at my face. He is gulping down a bottle of water. I watch him for a few minutes. He doesn't know what to say. I wish I could tell him I'm going to be okay, but most of all I wish the bottle of water was mine. My mouth is so dry.

'Daddy loves you, Clodagh. Daddy loves you.'

He is looking around frantically. His eyes are bloodshot. I feel my heart break as I look at his broken face. He clearly can't think of anything else to say. 'Your mother will be here in a minute,' he says. 'She popped out for a cup of tea. She's getting one for me too.'

I watch him drink the water. I wish I could gulp down a glass of water like I did after a long run. I want to scream at him, *Stop saying you love me! Please help me! You always fix everything. Please fix this!* My mouth doesn't seem to be making saliva, my sore tongue is furred and the breathing tube that is keeping my mouth open feels so heavy I fear it will crack my teeth.

I know that the IV drip beside my bed must keep me hydrated; but is it possible that without a drink I will die? Everyone who visits me is always carrying a bottle of water, gulping it down. It feels like a form of torture. There's no relief.

Almost worse is the fact that my mouth feels so dirty. My body is clean – a nurse undresses me and washes my body twice a day – but nobody has so much as looked into my mouth since I've been here. I'm always particular about my teeth; people comment on my nice white smile. I have no tooth decay. I clean

14

them several times a day. But now I can't even tell whether my breath smells. The thought really bothers me.

Mum comes back and hands Dad his tea. She looks at me warily, then sits down beside me. I want to hug her, tell her I'll be okay. They sit there on either side of my bed, worry etched on their faces. They both look so broken. I'm their little girl. They have always looked out for me, always made things better. They gave me a job in their shop when I first applied to the police and they kept turning me down. They helped me cope when my marriage ended. I could always rely on them for support, but there's not a thing they can do for me now.

It upsets me having them here. It's worse still seeing Dad slumped over, the picture of despair, when it's time for them to leave. But the worst thing, the very worst, is when I lie here alone. That's when the dark thoughts crowd in.

The days are endless. I watch the clock and the minute hand doesn't seem to move. Why does no one notice? I stare at it, counting out seconds, willing the time to pass. Time has slowed down. Five minutes feels like an hour.

I'm consumed by fear. I'm alive only because these machines are breathing for me. It would be so easy for a nurse to kill me by mistake. It could happen, couldn't it? A medical error. And then I'd be dead.

When they turn me onto my side for my bed-baths, I worry they will disconnect a vital tube. Often I feel the tug of the catheter between my legs, the needles in my hands and arms nipping my skin as I'm rolled from one side to the other. Sweat pours off me. It tickles my face, my body. I wish I could jump into a cold swimming pool. I'm terrified I'll die from overheating. Why does no one notice?

Every day I stare at the pepper-spattered ceiling tiles. Every day I watch the clock. Every day I watch the nurses as they flit around the ward, busying themselves with charts. The air is so still; I am so still. I will them to walk past my bed, just close enough for me to feel the air move for just a few seconds. The movement of the air around me for just a few seconds feels incredible, a brief relief from the stillness. Otherwise, I feel a constant, overwhelming sense of dread. Will this torture ever end?

I wish just one of the nurses would stop and chat to me, instead of gossiping among themselves about their lives, about where they went on Saturday night, about what they are wearing to an upcoming wedding. I hate their laughter and chatter. I'm not in on it. I want to scream at them to shut up. I want to say, *I'm on life support here! How can you be talking about weddings and nights out?*

The air doesn't move. I can't move. Why isn't there a window? I'd do anything for a bit of daylight. I'd love a view of something other than the ceiling. The lights hurt my eyes; the beep of machines irritates my ears. Everything irritates me. I can't wait to have the tube removed. Then I'll be able to talk.

When Adrian arrives and looks into my eyes my fear eases. I feel safe. I feel he can read my eyes and understand what I'm thinking. His visits make things better for a few hours. Somehow he knows when I'm uncomfortable and sponges the sweat from my brow. I try to savour the time with him but I know that when he leaves my torture will begin again. The sweat will start to run down my face again. That I can cope with, but when it starts to roll down my neck and behind my ears I just want to scream.

Adrian has spoken to the medical staff, but they've said that in the ICU their main concern is keeping me alive. They won't assess whether I can communicate or not until a speech-and-language therapist sees me – and that won't be until I'm moved from the ICU.

So, for now, Adrian helps me develop my blinks. The most crucial ones are one blink for yes, two for no. But we add three blinks for, 'I love you.'

'Is that enough?' he asks. I blink twice.

'No?' He strokes his beard in thought, then gives me a cheeky grin. 'How about four blinks for "You're a moron?"'

Perfect, I think. I blink once, wait for him to acknowledge it, then blink four times.

Adrian laughs, kisses me and says, 'Clodagh, you're a moron.' He pauses, then says, 'You are going to be okay.'

I blink three times.

I live for Adrian's visits. I love it when he places his hand softly on my fingers, avoiding the wires coming from my hand. I love when he carefully kisses my forehead when he arrives and before he leaves. But it's not enough. I want him to lie beside me and hug me. I want him to tell me when this is all going to end. I want him to tell me when I'm going to get better. I want to talk to him, to touch him. No one seems to want to touch me.

My parents seem frightened of all the wires and tubes. The ICU is alien to them. They live a nice life. They play golf, go out for dinner and nothing bad happens. I think seeing their daughter in ICU after a stroke is something they just can't process. They're worried that, if they touch me, they might break me. They might disturb something that's keeping me alive. Adrian, on the other hand, is used to seeing horrible, life-changing stuff at work – kids kneecapped, people dead in road-traffic collisions. This environment doesn't intimidate him.

He stays with me for as long as he can and, when he goes, I lie there, alone again with my thoughts, staring at the ceiling. I've always been in control of what Adrian and I eat. I'm worried that, without me at home with him, he'll eat junk food. He definitely won't get his five a day.

I think of him driving to the empty Forever House. I picture him standing alone in the kitchen, where we like to dance. It's cold and dark. He's staring into an empty fridge, his stomach groaning with hunger. He's lonely.

Night-time is the worst part of any 24 hours. I think of my life before the stroke. Like most people, I've had my ups and downs, but it was a good life on the whole. After I met Adrian and lived with him I was truly happy. Life felt perfect. And now I'm lying helpless, in a nappy, with a catheter draining my urine. Can life have been that good only for it now to be over?

As the days pass I learn the routine. The nurses wash me in the morning and they wash me in the evening. Bed-baths bring a rollercoaster of emotions. They frighten me. I am scared that, rolling me onto my side so my back can be washed, one of them will accidentally roll me too far. The bed is so narrow that they might just drop me onto the hard floor, which would disconnect my life support. I can't move – I wouldn't be able to break my fall. Instead I'd break every bone in my body.

On the other hand, I love the human touch. I love the coolness I feel as each limb is exposed. I love the way the water cools my skin and the freshness that follows. I love the fact that when they're washing me they talk to me, not over me; at least, most of them do.

They tell me what they are doing, and they ask if the temperature suits me. Some of them even go the extra mile. They mention Adrian, and tease me about how good-looking he is. They've learnt I'm a police officer. I wonder who told them. I've always kept my job private. But they say they admire the job I have and that it must be really interesting.

I try hard to show the nurses I love bed-bath time. It's one of the only highlights of my day, along with visiting time. It's the only time I'm not too hot. I try and smile. Can I smile? I don't know, but I try with all my might to move my mouth. When they ask me if I'm enjoying it, I always blink once: *yes!*

When the nurses finish, they stand back to check my positioning in the bed, but I am never comfortable. I'm sure they think I am. I must look serene and peaceful. I'm propped up well with pillows and my head is supported, but they don't notice that my nightdress is crumpled at the back. My heels and elbows burn from being in the same position for hours. I feel like my tail bone could burst through my skin. I could scream from the pain. I am only ever moved when I get a bed-bath.

I can almost cope with the burning pain, with the unbearable heat, but when I feel an itch and can't move to scratch it I fear I could lose my mind.

I can't work out how many beds are in intensive care, but my bed is opposite the nurses' station. I can hear a nurse talking on the phone. I hear my name mentioned. It's just after ten o'clock and I realise it's Adrian on the other end of the phone.

'Clodagh is fine,' I hear. 'We've made her comfortable for the night.'

But I'm not comfortable! I want to scream out. *I'm too hot! No one has looked at me to see that. How can you not see the sweat on my face?*

Every night feels like a Bear Grylls extreme survival challenge. Do I give up? Do I just lie there, not thinking, not trying to will any little part of me to move? Or do I keep fighting?

One night my bowels move and I watch the clock. I wait eight whole hours for someone to notice. It is only when the smell fills intensive care that someone comes and tracks it down to me.

'Clodagh, I think your bowels have moved,' she says. 'Let's get you cleaned.'

I know it's partly because I need someone to blame for the situation I'm in, but I feel so angry with the nurses. The simple fact that they can talk and move makes me jealous. I have no control over anything. I've just lain in my own excrement for eight hours there was nothing I could do about it.

Whenever someone is arrested and brought to the custody suite in a police station, their welfare is continually checked. We look in on a prisoner at least every hour. Even though there are cameras in the cells, we still carry out a physical check. Surely a patient on life support should be checked at least as often as a prisoner in a police station? The nurses seem to spend more time doing paperwork than looking after us.

Stop relying on the machines and just touch me! I want to scream at them. *Touch me and you'll feel I'm overheating!*

I'm in intensive care. With all the drips, the needles and the tubes coming from my mouth and arms, I'm smart enough to realise I must be fighting for my life. Are the nurses taking my condition as seriously as I think they should?

I stare at the ceiling. By now I know every inch of every tile above me. I need to keep myself sane somehow. I recite the crime definitions I learnt when training in the police college. I am sweating and I feel every droplet roll slowly across my face. Sweat drops into my eyes and stings. I wish I could change my position. I recently learned every article of the European Convention of Human Rights by heart for an exam at work. I recite sections now in my head. Having to lie in my own excrement is definitely degrading. Are my human rights being breached?

Every story has an end, though. Right now I am paralysed in intensive care, but I won't be forever. As each day passes, I keep telling myself, this *can't* last forever. Still, every day, the hours drag more than they did the day before. Twenty-four hours is difficult to fill when you can't move a muscle and the only thing you can do is stare at the ceiling tiles above you.

I try to use up the hours of the day by closing my eyes and choosing pictures or moments from my life to relive. My favourite memories are from my childhood, with Diane. I remember us twirling in matching dresses, dancing to Abba, riding our bicycles as fast as we could. I remember laughing until it hurt with KD in Barcelona. If I concentrate hard enough, I can almost hear Adrian's and my 'dance me' music.

One Saturday night is really dragging. I'm staring at the ceiling as usual, trying to choose a picture in my mind to pass the time. I hear a flurry of activity as a woman is brought into the bed next to mine. I hear the whoosh of the curtains being pulled. Listening to the talk from the doctors, I realise she is relatively young – the same age as me – but she is not expected to live. My heart beats faster in fear.

I listen intently to hear what has happened to her. From the pieces of conversation I pick up, she has tried to end her life by hanging. I feel helpless. I think of times when I had to help people who were suicidal when I was on duty. I always felt sad when people decided that death was a better choice than life.

They're fighting hard to keep her alive. That's obvious from the heightened tension in their voices, from the bulges in the curtain as they work on her. There is a lull in activity. I will her to stay alive.

'Okay. We've done what we can,' says a voice. 'The family can come in and see her.'

I hear barely suppressed crying as the woman's family gather around her bed, asking each other why. When they're asked to leave so that the team can carry out some procedures and checks, I listen to the sound of their crying fade into the distance.

When the family are allowed in again, a priest comes with them. I hear him murmuring the last rites. I don't want to hear him. I don't want to hear any of this. I don't want her to die. Her family are frantic and can't keep the volume of their crying down. I want this to stop. I want to scream. I try to cry but, of course, I make no sound. No one notices me.

I am sorry for your loss, I want to say. *It is so awful what has happened. How could someone's world end like this when life is so beautiful?* I yearn to give them a hug. But all I can do is stare at the ceiling and the glimpse of blue curtain.

I really hope she is at peace.

The family leave and I hear medical staff return. I listen to their chatter. They aren't doing anything wrong. Not really. But inside I'm thinking, *Stop talking! This woman has died. She is the same age as me. Everything has to stop.*

It doesn't seem fair this family's world has come to a crashing halt and everything else continues on as normal. The world should pause, if only for a minute. What will the nurses talk about when I am dying? Because I might. It could happen at any moment.

The next night a new nurse comes onto the ward.

'Hi Clodagh, I'm Alma,' she says. 'I live near you.' Giving me my bed-bath, sponging me down so gently, she asks if I would like her to wash my hair. I blink: *yes*. Rinsing off the shampoo, she describes the road where she lives, and in my head, I say, *That's near where my parents have a shop. You must know them.*

Alma seems to know what I want without being told. Realising I am hot, she positions two fans to make sure cool air is blowing on me.

'Is that good, Clodagh?'

I blink once.

'Would you like a cold compress for your head? You're burning up.'

Again I blink once – and thank Adrian in my head for telling the nurses about my blinks. As Alma flits about the ward, I drift in and out of sleep. Watching Alma through half-closed eyes, she looks like a red-haired angel. I'm almost sure I can see wings!

It's just as well that I've had a restful night, because the next day proves challenging. The doctors come around in the morning and, after asking me how I am, they say, 'Clodagh, we're going to remove the tube from your mouth. We want to see if you can breathe by yourself. Is that okay?'

I blink once, but I feel nervous. What if I can't? But I want to be able to talk, so it's best to remove it. There is a whooshing of curtains. Uniformed people stand around my bed, each of them staring at me. The doctor in charge positions himself behind my head. He removes the pillow my head is resting on. I am lying completely flat. I stare at the ceiling tiles. Both his hands are on my cheeks. They move across to my chin. The movement nips my skin. He must be wearing latex gloves.

Slowly, bit by bit, I feel the tube edge out of my throat. A face with gloved hands is holding the growing length of tube. I don't like this. The doctor's voice interrupts my thoughts: 'Breathe, Clodagh, breathe.'

I try. But as I lie staring at the ceiling, I can't make anything happen. My mind races. I thought I'd gasp, but I can't take even the tiniest inward breath. I panic. I can't breathe. *I can't breathe!* I stare in panic at the faces around me. They stare back at me and don't move. Are they going to stand there and watch me die?

Just when I'm convinced I'm about to suffocate, a mask is shoved on my face. Someone frantically squeezes a bag attached to the mask and pumps air into my mouth. I'm terrified. I can feel the air being forced into my mouth, but it's not filling my lungs. Everyone is blurring. My world is turning black.

I open my eyes. It's like the first day again. The tube is back and my tongue hurts. I can't believe this has happened to me. Did I really almost die just now? *I need to tell Adrian about this*, I think. A nurse is watching my monitors. The other faces have gone.

I watch the clock, willing it to reach two o'clock, visiting time. My parents arrive first. Every day I see them my heart breaks a little more. I hate seeing them so sad. Sitting down, I know my mum doesn't know what to say. There is silence.

'How are you today, pet?' Why does Mum have to talk so loudly? Just because I can't move or talk, does she think I'm deaf? 'Diane's coming later.'

I like seeing Diane. She's not afraid to touch me and she talks more about what has happened to me than anyone. She treats me as me. She wipes the sweat from my face and makes sure to put lip balm on my cracked lips. She tells me I'm on a journey of recovery, but I will make it to the end.

The last time she visited, she filled in my missing hours. She hadn't wanted to upset me before that. She said she was in denial, too – she couldn't believe it all wasn't a bad dream.

'The doctors in A & E thought it was meningitis,' she told me. 'I felt so hopeless. They didn't scan you. I couldn't understand why. I was convinced you had a brain tumour and I pleaded with them to do it. If they didn't, I said, I knew you would die.'

Eventually they listened to her. And the news was not good.

'They came in, looking sheepish, and told me that you had a clot in your brainstem. They said, "We don't know if she will make it."'

That's when they arranged the transfer to the Royal. They sent me there so that they could retrieve the clot. And by that time, early on Tuesday morning, Adrian had arrived back from Scotland.

I have my eyes closed as I remember her words. Then Dad brings me back to the present.

'Daddy loves you, Clodagh.'

Yes, I think. *I know. You've been telling me that all my life.*

I feel angry with the doctors and nurses. They wouldn't believe that I was ill. Now my dad has to watch his daughter on life support. I feel angry because his face is so grey and my illness might just kill him. He's my dad and he shouldn't have to see me like this.

Mum doesn't know what to do with herself. She is twitching my sheet, trying to make it straight. Then Adrian walks in. I'm pleased to see him, but he looks at my mother like she's a constable who has just given him poor paperwork. Mum looks like Adrian's arrival at my bedside just might make her release the tears she has been holding back.

He kisses my forehead, then says hello to Mum and Dad, who say hello back. Adrian and I have been in a relationship for two years. But he and my parents haven't yet got to know each other very well. Now this awful situation has forced them together. And it's clear that something has happened between them.

Minutes pass. The three remain at my bedside, not moving, as if they're scared of what will happen next. Mum breaks the uneasy silence.

'I could do with a cup of coffee,' she says, standing up and gathering her belongings. Dad continues to sit there, hands in his lap. She glares at him, so he stands up and follows her out of the ward.

What has happened? I want to scream. Adrian lets out a sigh.

'Clodagh,' he says, 'this is so tough!'

I blink four times, to try and lighten the mood.

'I know your parents love you, Clodagh, and they only want the best for you. And I know that you and I have only been together two years. But do you know what your mother said as we were leaving yesterday?'

I blink twice for no.

'She said, "Don't you hurt her."' He shook his head. 'She sounded so fierce. She honestly thought that because of what has happened I would walk away and leave you.' He pauses. 'Diane was there too, and she said nothing, like that was an okay thing for your mother to say. What do they think I am?'

He sits there, his head in his hands, looking defeated. I look at him.

She's my mother, I want to tell him. *She's looking out for me. She doesn't mean anything by saying that.* I wish I could talk.

'I was so annoyed,' he says. 'Do they not realise that we have a built a life together?' He sighs again. 'I turned around to your mother and said, "You have more chance of hurting Clodagh than I do." And I walked off.' He twists my thumb ring around in agitation. 'What type of person do they think I am?'

I'm furious with Adrian. Furious that this has happened. Furious he has my thumb ring. What did he mean by telling my mother she had more chance of hurting me than him? I know Adrian won't leave. He is my partner and I am his. I glare at him. He doesn't understand.

He will be able to process whatever the doctors are saying, but I know that my parents simply can't understand how their fit, active, healthy daughter has had a stroke. Even I am struggling to understand it. He needs to understand that my mum's world has fallen apart. I've been her daughter for 35 years. He has only been in my life for two. To me her concerns are logical. He's being over-sensitive.

I wish I could explain that to Adrian, but I can't, so I blink four times.

You're all morons.

Adrian laughs. He sits in silence for a while, letting his anger settle. Then, standing up, he leans over and holds both my forearms as he stares into my eyes.

'Clodagh, I love you. We will get through this together. We will beat this together. I know it!'

I believe him. I *have* to believe him – because this simply can't be forever.

I blink three times.

It's night. I pray that Alma the angel will be on duty again, but she isn't. It's a pretty young nurse who comes up with a bowl of water, ready to give me my bed-bath. She smiles, then whooshes the curtains around. She's chatty. I like her.

'Clodagh,' she says, 'my mum had a stroke a couple of months ago.'

I stare at her, waiting to hear what she was going to tell me about her mum.

'She's doing very well. She's back at her Zumba classes now. You'll be back on your feet before long.'

I would love to believe her, but I know that whatever kind of stroke the nurse's mother had, it isn't as bad as mine. I must believe that I will recover – yet I'm beginning to realise that my stroke was more severe than most. After all, it's affected every part of my body – on the left side and the right. And why have I not yet regained any movement at all? Surely there should have been some improvement by now?

Half of me is in despair; the other half is positive. But even that positive side is starting to think that I might not get to dance at my friend Fiona's wedding, and that is six weeks away.

I met Fiona when she joined the police service; I trained her when she was a probationer constable. She is a beautiful person, inside and out. Bubbly, with long brown hair and blue eyes, but not at all sporty like me. She's a girly girl. We're very different, but maybe that's why we get along together so well.

In the past few weeks, wanting to get fit before her wedding, Fiona joined me in the gym. We exercised together and she complained that I made her do terrible exercises. I laughed. Damien, her husband-to-be, sometimes joined us. He also wanted to get fit before the wedding. He ran beside me on the treadmill.

'God, Clodagh, how do you find this fun?' he said. But we did have fun.

Thinking of the wedding makes me remember a dress I saw in a boutique – a mint-green skirt with a black-and-white bodice. It was stunning, but how can I tell Adrian to go and buy it for me? If I don't, and soon, it probably won't be available in my size. It's all very well being able to blink for yes and no, but without speech how will I ever manage to communicate anything else? The frustration of it nearly drives me demented.

I'll just have to wear something I already own, I think.

And what about shoes? I have some beautiful black heels – they're new. But will I be able to walk in them? Some people who have a stroke end up with a limp. Perhaps I should wear gladiator sandals instead, but Adrian will have to buy them for me too. With nothing but blinks to work with, I'll never get him to understand!

I feel sad. I face facts. I won't be doing Zumba classes any time soon. There is nothing – nothing in the world – I love as much as dancing at a wedding, but I definitely won't be dancing at Fiona and Damien's wedding. In fact, I might never dance again.

Fiona has seen the dress. We drove past the boutique on what turned out to be my last day of work. April Fools' Day.

CHAPTER FOUR

April Fools' Day

Wednesday, 1 April started like any other day. Adrian was in Scotland, having physiotherapy at a rehabilitation centre. He'd injured his back in a car accident at work. With our different shifts, though, it wasn't unusual for me to be alone.

I was on the night shift so I had the day to myself. I slept until lunchtime. Bleary eyed, I went for a run, sticking to my usual route. It's four-and-a-half miles on narrow, hilly, country roads. I pushed myself, trying to beat the pace Adrian and I normally run at. Without Adrian, I had an opportunity to set a new record for the route. I am fiercely competitive. I wanted to be able to tell Adrian I'd managed a new and faster time.

I wasn't due on duty until 11 o'clock. This was an overtime shift I'd volunteered to do for a colleague, so I wouldn't be with my normal response team. I didn't mind. Adrian and I had grand plans for the Forever House and an extra shift would mean extra money.

I ran into the briefing room two minutes late, which is quite normal for me. As I perched myself on a desk, I was pleased to see Fiona there. She was part of my usual team and, when the sergeant detailed the two of us in a crew for the night with Davy, I was pleased. Davy is a gentleman and a good crew makes for a nicer shift. Besides, I'd get a chat during the night with Fiona. I suggested that Fiona should drive for the first part of the shift.

'I'll take over at one,' I said. 'We can rotate for the night.'

'Sounds good to me,' she said.

I had some paperwork to finish from my last duty. The second half of the night, when tiredness kicks in and it's a struggle to stay awake, makes even the simplest of paperwork nearly impossible. I always liked to get everything perfect, but spelling perfectly at four o'clock in the morning is challenging.

Our duty, when not completing paperwork, was to patrol around the city in armoured cars, to look for anything unusual and to respond to 999 calls. It could be anything – burglaries, criminal damage, road-traffic collisions or assaults. And, with the city having a severe terror-threat level, we sometimes had to stop and search vehicles and people for items intended for use in terrorism. Attending the scene of a paramilitary shooting and standing at the cordon point of a suspected bomb were not unusual duties for us.

Responding to 999 emergency calls is an exciting job; but even routine calls can lead to danger. Police officers are always a target for dissident republicans. Colleagues have had devices thrown at their cars as they've patrolled and shots fired at them when responding to calls. I was so used to having the words 'RUC whore' shouted at me, I almost didn't hear them any more.

After saying goodbye to Fiona and Davy, I headed to the night kitchen. I made some tea and chatted to a few colleagues who were exhausted after a busy shift. Their flak jackets and patrol bags lay abandoned on the floor. I didn't need to put on my gear just yet. I would go and start my paperwork. Running up the three flights of stairs, I went into the constables' workroom and sat down at a computer.

My phone made me jump when it abruptly vibrated at exactly one o'clock. It was a text from Fiona, asking if I was ready to take over the driving.

'Give me five,' I texted. I needed to collect my flak jacket and patrol belt from the locker room and visit the bathroom. I made my way to the women's toilets, swiping my pass and entering the code to gain access through the security doors along the corridor.

I was washing my hands when suddenly my body felt like jelly. A wave of nausea surged through me. I felt hot; the bathroom began to spin. I fell to the ground.

'Am I dying?' I thought. 'What is wrong with me? I can't die on the floor of the toilets in a police station!'

I needed to get help.

But I couldn't get up. The room was revolving around me. I felt frightened. I dragged myself back into the corridor, swallowing repeatedly, trying not to vomit. But the corridor was pitch black. There wasn't a soul around. A large, empty police-station building at night is an eerie place at the best of times, but now it was terrifying. I couldn't reach to swipe my pass. I felt my pockets for my mobile phone, then realised I'd left it back in the toilets, sitting on the sink. I don't know how I did it, but somehow I crawled back into the bathroom and reached up for the phone. Then the spinning room became too much and I fell on my back.

How do you type your password into your mobile phone when you can't see the screen and the room will not stop turning? I got it wrong once, then twice. Then sickness took over, and, crawling into the toilet cubicle, I vomited again and again. Would anyone find me tonight in the bathroom?

'Right, Clodagh,' I told myself, 'this is your last try for the password. If you get it wrong again, the phone will lock you out and you won't get help – you'll be dead.'

Somehow, I managed it. Relief swept over me as a familiar voice came on the line.

'Hello.' I instantly recognised Ray's voice. 'Communications.'

'Ray, it's Clodagh.'

'Hi, Clodagh.'

'I'm in the toilets on the third floor in the station.'

'Yes?' He sounded confused.

'I need help. I'm dying.' Then, as another wave of nausea surged through me, I dropped the phone. I put my head into the toilet bowl as my body continued to empty my stomach.

I don't know how long it was before Fiona ran into the bathroom, the duty sergeant following behind her, but by the time they arrived the fog in my brain seemed to be clearing. The spinning in the bathroom had stopped. If I hadn't been sitting on the toilet floor with vomit visible on my trousers, I might have seemed almost normal.

'What's wrong, darling?' Fiona sounded panicked.

'I don't know.'

I laughed, feeling embarrassed to have phoned communications to say that I was dying. How dramatic! 'I don't know what happened. One minute I was fine; the next I'd collapsed. I just felt that I was dying.' Looking at their still-worried faces, I said, 'Please, just help me up, would you?'

I expected to be able to spring straight up again, but the minute they helped me move the room began to revolve again and the nausea struck. It kept happening. I couldn't make it onto my feet. The duty sergeant used his police radio to ask communications to task an ambulance. I felt annoyed at him. Now *he* was the one being dramatic.

I was still in my vomit-soiled uniform when two paramedics arrived and helped me onto a stretcher. I had met them both, many times, at the scene of road-traffic collisions, or whenever there had been a sudden death. It felt strange to be the one needing their help. Wrapping me snugly in a white blanket, they carried me down three flights of stairs to the ambulance waiting in the station yard, next to the parked police cars. This was easier said than done, because movement – any movement at all – caused me to retch.

Fiona stepped into the ambulance.

'Darling, I'm coming with you,' she announced. I was relieved. As the medics did their bit, attaching me to various monitors, I began to cry. I vomited again and Fiona held a kidney-shaped cardboard container to my mouth.

We left the station in a dramatic flourish, blue lights flashing. Occasionally the sirens sounded as we sped across the city on our way to the hospital. I recalled how, as a child, I had dreamt of joining the police service. It wasn't only because my uncle was a policeman – the lure of flashing lights and blaring sirens had attracted me too. It was ironic, now, to know that the sirens rang out for my benefit. The journey took less than five minutes but my continuous retching made it feel longer. Finally, the ambulance rolled up at the entrance to A & E.

Part of me felt embarrassed as I was wheeled into the emergency department, my uniform identifying me as a police officer. I recognised some of the nursing staff from the times I'd been here as part of my duties. But I was here now on my own behalf, sick and crying, and that made me feel vulnerable.

I was given privacy – blue curtains were drawn around the cubicle they took me to. They inserted an IV drip into my arm, gave me anti-nausea medication, told me to try and sleep, and left me with only the beep of the monitoring machines and Fiona for company.

How could I sleep? I couldn't. I was frightened. What was wrong with me? Did I have a brain tumour?

'Do you want to phone Adrian?' asked Fiona, seeing that I was awake. Although I wished he could be with me in A & E, and would have loved to hear his voice, I said no. It wasn't fair to wake him in the middle of the night while he was in Scotland; and, when I didn't know what was wrong with me, what was the point? I'd ring him once I knew what was wrong.

But, by morning, I was no nearer to finding that out. Although the nausea had gone away, I still wasn't right. I felt that if I moved too quickly I would collapse again. And that was worrying me.

'What's the time?' I asked Fiona.

'Just after six.'

'Okay. I think I'll ring Adrian now.'

She passed me my phone. He answered, his voice sounding gravelly. I'd obviously woken him from a deep sleep.

I told him that I was in A & E, that I felt ill but wasn't injured. He assured me that I was in the very best place, and mustn't worry.

'I'll come home if you want me to,' he said.

He talked on, sounding completely logical and reassuring. It was precisely what I needed to hear and hearing him talk made me feel a little better. But when, an hour later, a young doctor examined me and said I was now free to go home, I was worried. I felt like it all was going to happen again. Something in my head wasn't right. I didn't want to go home.

'Come back at two o'clock,' she said. 'You can see a neurologist then. They will do some further checks.'

'I don't feel back to normal,' I said. 'I'm worried that whatever happened last night will happen again – when I'm driving home.' But the young doctor had already walked out of our cubicle. Had she heard me? Had she chosen not to?

A patrol car drove into the ambulance bay at the entrance door of A & E to pick Fiona and me up and take us back to the station. The sun had risen. We'd spent almost the entire night shift at the hospital. Once in the car, I phoned my mum and explained the events of the past few hours.

'Can you or Dad collect me from work, please, and then bring me into hospital at two o'clock?'

She sounded busy.

'Sorry, pet,' she said. 'Diane is working today and I'm looking after Emily, Adam and Hannah. And your dad is working too.' I had forgotten that Diane would be at work today.

It was the last straw. Hanging up, I turned to Fiona.

'They can't come.'

I started to cry uncontrollably. I just couldn't manage the drive home.

'Clodagh, don't.' She put her hand on my arm. 'I can drive you home in your car and Damien can follow behind in ours. It's not a problem.'

'Thank you, Fi,' I said, just grateful that she and Damien had been on overtime too.

Fiona is always bright and happy. She sees no badness in the world. I always found it a little ironic that she chose to be a police officer. As she drove me home, she chatted about her upcoming wedding.

'I'm not sure whether to wear my hair up or down,' she said. 'What do you think?'

I was so tired that it took me a few seconds to realise she had asked me a question.

'I think down.' She has long brown hair and I knew she would look beautiful whatever she decided.

'I know what I want to wear,' I said. 'I'll show you when we drive past the shop.' We were just approaching my home town. 'There,' I said a few minutes later, pointing to a boutique at the corner of the main shopping area. In the window was a beautiful mint-green dress with a wide skirt and a black-and-white bodice. 'I spied it a few weeks ago. I love it – very Sarah Jessica Parker.'

'It's beautiful. You have to get it.' Glancing at me, she smiled, then she negotiated the roundabout. Looking sideways at Fiona, thinking how pretty she was, I knew she'd be a beautiful bride. I closed my eyes. We'd be home soon and

I couldn't wait to get to bed.

When we arrived home, Damien pulled up behind us and the two of them helped me in through the back door.

'This is lovely, Clodagh,' said Fiona, looking around my kitchen.

'Thanks,' I said. 'I'd love to give you a tour, Fi, but …' I tried to smile.

'Not now, I know. When you're feeling better. Would you like me to help you get ready for bed?'

I shook my head.

'I'm fine. Thanks so much for everything, Fi. You and Damien are amazing friends.'

'You'd have done the same. Text me later, let me know how you are feeling.'

She waved. They walked to their car and drove off. The minute they'd gone, I regretted letting them leave. My body felt like it had during the night and turned to jelly again. Feeling dizzy and nauseous, I crawled along the hallway to our bedroom, as though crawling through mud.

Why did I have to be so independent? Would it have killed me to ask Fiona and Damien to help me to bed? Reaching the bedroom, I glanced at the pyjamas folded on my pillow, thinking I should put them on. Then I pulled myself into bed in my vomit-stained uniform, keeping my heavy black patrol boots on, and fell into unconsciousness.

When I awoke my head felt clearer. I slipped out of bed and stood up slowly. There was a slight wooziness but, provided I moved really slowly, I seemed fine. I thought of driving myself into hospital for the checks – but suppose the spinning came back again. Worried, I rang my cousin Amanda, and, explaining the situation, asked her to drive me, just in case. She's a primary-school teacher, so she was off for the Easter holidays.

She arrived in time to help me get dressed. When she passed me shoes, I said, 'Not those. Just pass me my trainers.' She did. Everything felt difficult. It took all my energy to tie my laces. 'What's wrong with me?' I asked her. She shrugged.

'That's what we're going to find out.'

We arrived at the hospital, ten minutes early, and went to the neurology department. We waited. The appointment time came and went. Finally, the neurologist appeared. Calling me in, he started to examine me. I had thought I would be given scans, but the tests he performed seemed basic, to say the least.

'Clodagh, can you follow my finger with your eyes, please?' I did that. Then he stared into my eyes with a pen torch. Next, he checked my pulse and blood pressure and tested my limbs for signs of weakness. I had to hold up my arms, then my legs, and after that he checked my balance.

'That seems fine,' he said, and turned to his desk, where he jotted down some notes. Then he gave me my diagnosis.

'You've had an unexplained lack of consciousness.'

'What does that mean?'

'You won't be able to drive for the next 12 months.' He made the statement as though he were asking someone to boil the kettle. But, of course, this would have a huge impact on my everyday life.

'I drive to work every day. I drive *at* work. You can't tell me what's wrong with me, but you can give me a driving ban for a year?'

He shrugged.

'I'll consult with another neurologist.' He left the room and returned with a colleague, who asked a few questions and then said, 'Don't drive for the next 24 hours.'

'I'm due to fly to Scotland tomorrow,' I said. I was joining Adrian for the weekend. 'It's an evening flight. Does that mean I'm okay to drive myself to the airport ...' I calculated, 'in 28 hours?'

He nodded and, rising to his feet, showed me the door.

'Are you sure I'm okay? I feel like, if I do anything strenuous, I will have another episode.'

'If you do, you can return to hospital,' he said in a dismissive tone.

'That's good. Nothing serious,' said Amanda as she drove me home.

I nodded, but I still felt uneasy. Something wasn't right.

The following morning, Good Friday, I sat in the kitchen, nursing a cup of tea. My head felt as if was stuffed with cotton wool. I couldn't think straight and my limbs felt heavy. Again, walking was like moving through mud. When my phone rang and I heard Adrian's voice on the line, I began to cry hysterically.

'There *is* something wrong with me!' I could barely get the words out through my loud sobbing. 'Whatever that doctor says. He told me I'm fine to drive this afternoon, but I just can't.'

'Don't, then. Don't come to Scotland,' he said. 'Rest up at home for the weekend.'

I could hear the disappointment in his voice and, in truth, I was sure he was thinking I was being overdramatic. He'd never seen me cry and never heard me hysterical. I was his GI Jane – iron willed, not someone who gave in to illness. Getting myself together and calming down, I said, 'It's okay. I'll get my parents to drive me.'

'That's great! I'll collect you at the airport. And we needn't *do* anything much. We can have a relaxing weekend.'

The minute I walked through arrivals and saw Adrian standing there, holding a sign with my name on it, I laughed. I knew I'd done the right thing. I walked towards Adrian. He was smiling at me. My head still felt like it was stuffed with cotton wool but, when he gave me a tight hug, I began to feel a bit better.

We drove to the rehab centre. Adrian talked about the physiotherapy he had had during the week. His back was feeling better. He had booked dinner in a nice Indian restaurant and, after dinner, we went for a walk. I didn't know if it was the coolness of the night air, the peacefulness of the centre or just holding Adrian's hand as we walked, but I felt completely myself again.

The next morning we set off for Stirling Castle. We walked up the hill. When we reached the top I dropped to the ground. The cotton-wool feeling in my head had returned.

'I think I'm going to pass out,' I said.

Adrian sat beside me, his arm around me. I was glad he was there – someone who knew me, who knew how unlike me this was. Now he would see that I wasn't overreacting. When we got back to the centre, Adrian took me straight to a nurse to get checked out. My pulse and blood pressure were fine, but I wasn't altogether reassured. I still felt strange and the cotton-wool feeling in my head was getting worse. I went to bed for a few hours.

Changing into a dress and my favourite heels for dinner, I felt miserable. I had planned an active, fun weekend, but now I felt like a killjoy. As we waited for our main course to arrive, something lifted. My head was suddenly clear; the cotton-wool feeling gone. In a split second I felt better. I was me again. I remained well for the rest of the visit. I felt carefree.

Leaving me back to Glasgow Airport, Adrian said sternly, 'Don't go back on Monday for that week of nights. You've been working a lot of hours – all those long shifts with overtime. Add in all your running and all those hours in the gym. You're not right, Clodagh, I can tell. And whatever it is – even if it's only tiredness or a virus – you can certify yourself off work for a week, then go back feeling fresh.'

'But I *never* take time off,' I said.

Adrian glared at me. He spoke to me in the Sergeant Simpson voice he knew I hated.

'Suppose you go in on Monday night, thinking you're going to have a quiet night, you're detailed driver of the crew and you come over faint again. It's not just you in the car if you crash, you know. Stop being stubborn. Just take the week off.'

'Maybe,' I said, kissing him on the lips. 'I'll let you know when I get home safe.'

'I'll see you on Friday.' He hugged me tightly. Then, waving at him, I went through to security, turning around for a last glimpse.

When he was out of sight, I hit a wall of loneliness.

CHAPTER FIVE

There Was a Bomb in My Head

I always wanted to be a police officer. My mum once found an old school jotter in the attic belonging to me. It's there in my childhood handwriting from when I was seven years old. It says it in black and white: 'When I grow up, I want to be a police officer.'

My uncle was in the police – he was a constable – and everyone always had great things to say about him. He was murdered by the IRA in 1976, three years before I was born – ambushed on a routine patrol with two colleagues. He was only 30 years old, younger than I am now. I remember hearing how my aunt, his young widow, had clung to his bloodstained body in the mortuary.

I thought of him as a brave, handsome man who saved people and did wonderful things. I romanticised his death in my head and compared him to a Marvel superhero. I wanted to be exactly like him, helping people and saving lives.

But Dad had other ideas for my future.

'Being a police officer is a dangerous job, Clodagh, and it's definitely no job for a woman,' he said. But if someone tells me not to do something – especially if they're dismissive – it makes me more determined to do it.

I was born during the Northern Ireland conflict – but, apart from my uncle's death, the Troubles didn't touch my life very deeply. I saw the aftermath of a bomb in the town centre once, and there was an occasion when the house next door to us was targeted with a nail-bomb and a drive-by shooting, but I never had to live in fear like some people.

At 18 I told my parents I was joining the police.

'Go to university first,' they said. I agreed, somewhat reluctantly, and went off to university to study history and politics. I was happy, but I have to admit that the biggest achievement of my time spent there was learning to recognise a nice bottle of white wine.

I met my best friend there, too – Karen, otherwise known as KD. We were opposites. She was studious, earning a first-class degree in law; I was laid back and easy going, just happy to graduate. But, despite our different attitudes to study, we became inseparable.

I travelled after university – to America, then around the world. On my return from my adventures, I applied for the police. I got a rejection. I hadn't scored highly enough in the rigorous assessments. I was disappointed, but agreed to work in Mum and Dad's furniture shop to pass the time until I could apply again. I enjoyed it. We had regulars who would call in – with no intention of buying furniture. I'd put on the kettle, they'd drink tea and we'd sit and talk for hours. I loved listening to their stories. I knew that half of them weren't true, but they were always interesting.

To escape the legacy of the Troubles, the Good Friday Agreement created a new police service. There was a need to rebalance the service in order to represent the whole community. Recruitment was to be delivered in line with what was commonly known as '50–50 legislation'. For every Protestant recruited, a member of the Catholic community had to be recruited too. A huge number of people wanted to be part of this new beginning. The new service processed over 100,000 applications for only 4,000 appointments. This made it difficult to get accepted. But I was determined to become a police officer. I kept applying and, on the seventh attempt, I got in.

The delay made me determined to be the very best I could be. I was, and am, a perfectionist when it comes to police work. Adrian would say I'm the same with everything. I loved police college and did my best to excel. On graduation day I won a prize in every category. I looked down into the audience and searched for my parents.

When I ran down after the graduation ceremony, saying, 'I didn't think I would have done this well,' Dad said, 'You did brilliant, pet.' I was delighted. Then, in his next breath, he said, 'Just think. If you had worked as hard as that in school, who knows where you'd be now?'

I stopped and glared at him.

'But I'm where I want to be!'

'You could have been anything.'

I felt like hitting him but I knew he was just worried about me. He wanted to make sure I came to no harm. He'd lost his brother-in-law to the police service. The last thing he wanted was to lose his daughter too.

Later, drinking tea with Mum, she told me what I wanted to hear.

'I'm so proud of you. Your dad will miss you in the shop. You're the son he never had. He wants the world for you and Diane. You're his little girls. Always will be.'

I loved being a police officer. All those times when I was the driver on duty, responding to 999 calls with sirens sounding and blue lights flashing. I loved the thrill of it. The fact that I was flirting with danger added an extra element of adrenaline. I never worried about dying. In an armoured car, with my patrol kit and colleagues beside me, I never really felt unsafe. Occasionally there would be a call that would make me stop and think about the dangers, but even then I didn't lose sleep about them. I was naïve.

I had one of those close calls just a month before my stroke. On a Sunday-night shift, my crew and I were driving out to a housing estate in the city to respond to an ongoing burglary. There'd been a 999 call but, just as we were approaching the scene, communications shouted into our earpieces, telling us to withdraw immediately. It turned out to have been a hoax call, designed to lure us in. A pressure-pad bomb had been placed at the side of the house we were heading for. The bomb would have gone off as soon as an officer stood on it.

I didn't spend too much time thinking about days like that. I did sometimes worry about Adrian putting himself in danger, though. His current car bore bomb damage. He'd been the duty sergeant on a night when dissident republicans had attacked the station. They had hijacked a local taxi, forcing the driver to drive to the station with 200 pounds of home-made explosives on board. The bombers abandoned the taxi at the front gate. There were three people queuing for kebabs in the takeaway opposite the station. Without a second thought, Adrian sprinted past the car with the bomb in it to warn them and lead them to safety. The bomb exploded soon later, 23 minutes after the police had received a coded warning saying that they had 45 minutes to clear the area.

It caused enormous damage to the station, the surrounding buildings and Adrian's car, but thanks to his courage no lives were lost. He was hailed as a hero in the local news. Would I have had the guts to run towards a bomb to save someone? Would I have been that brave? I like to think I would. Maybe, one day, I'll have the chance to find out.

If only I had known that Sunday night, back then, that the greatest danger to my life wasn't a terrorist bomb. All that time there was a weakness in the artery of my neck – an old minor injury sustained in a road-traffic collision. By pulling my heavy flak jacket over my head every day, I had never given the injury a chance to heal. In fact, it had slowly got worse.

All that time, there was a bomb in my head. It was already ticking. And it chose Easter Monday to explode.

I felt good when I woke up the morning after my return from Scotland, and the day started well. Waking to sunshine, I put on my shorts and a vest top, ready for a run. I felt 100 per cent better and I intended to run a half-marathon distance, 13 miles. I loved long runs but Adrian didn't. He would never do them with me. Now he was away, I would take the opportunity to do one by myself.

As I was blending fruits and seeds for my breakfast smoothie I glanced out of the window, thankful that it was a beautiful day. But the sunlight showed water spots, from rain and snow during the winter, on the outside of the windows – and I realised it was months since I had cleaned them. I kicked off my purple trainers and went to get my flip-flops. I'd run tomorrow.

I cleaned the windows and, feeling very productive, put on music and sang at the top of my voice, glad there was nobody there to hear me. Windows finished, I turned my attention to the inside of the house. As I worked, I thought back to the events of the previous Wednesday night and wondered if I had overreacted. Clearly I was fine!

I'm a perfectionist around the house. Diane says it's not normal but I like everything clean and in its place. By teatime the inside of the house was sparkling. I had a shower; then, in fresh shorts and T-shirt, my hair hanging damply down my back, I lay down on our corner sofa and switched on the TV. I'd watch a movie.

Diane had left me an Easter egg and I ate the lot. As I finished the last piece of chocolate, I noticed Diane's car pull up at our gate, above me on the road. I reluctantly dragged myself off the sofa, because, feeling lazy, I didn't want to get up and push the button to open the electric gates.

As I stood up and hit the button, that feeling – just like the one I had at work – came over me again. I felt like I was dying. My legs were like jelly and everything was spinning. I panicked, trying to work out if I could get to the back door in time to unlock it. I tried to run, terrified I wouldn't get there in time. I was falling; my legs were buckling beneath me. I managed it, somehow, and saw Diane standing there. Then I fell to the ground.

'Diane, Diane! Will you please ring an ambulance? Ring 999. I'm dying!' Terrified she would think I was messing about, I said, 'I'm not joking. Please, I'm serious!'

Diane stepped over me as I lay on the floor at the back door. Relief swept over me when I heard her say, 'My sister has collapsed.' Her voice was breaking. 'Her speech isn't right. It's slurred. And she's deathly white. I think she's having a stroke.'

She squatted beside me. I could see she was fighting back tears. 'They are on their way.' And, slowly, the dreadful sensation in my head eased.

Diane helped me to sit up.

'That's strange,' I said. 'I feel better now.'

'Well, you don't look right.'

I felt unsteady as she pulled me to my feet and supported me as I walked to the sofa. But then, watching the sun disappear beneath the horizon, I felt completely normal. Maybe Adrian was right – I just needed a few more days off.

Diane's husband, David, wandered in with Emily, Adam and Hannah.

'You left us in the car!' the eldest, Emily, moaned. I smiled at them and was about to suggest that Diane call the emergency services again and say it was a false alarm when blue flashing lights approached in the driveway.

Diane went to the front door and led two paramedics into the living room.

'I feel a bit embarrassed,' I said as they entered the room. 'I'm okay now.'

Checking my pulse and my blood pressure, asking me to follow his finger with my eyes, the taller paramedic, crouching beside me, hooked me up to various machines and asked me what I thought had happened.

'This sounds really silly, but it felt as if I was having a stroke.' I laughed, because I was too young for that.

'We'll take you to A & E to get checked out.'

Diane rushed off to pack an overnight bag. Then she bounded into the ambulance.

'David will take Emily, Adam and Hannah home. I'll come with you.'

'I'm fine, Di. I don't need an overnight bag. I won't be staying.'

'Well, just in case, you wally, better to have it.' Diane gave me a cheeky smile.

'Where do you work?' It was the larger paramedic. I thought of denying my job. For security reasons I always tell people that I'm a civil servant, but I had given some police teddy bears to Emily, Adam and Hannah, gifts from my trip at the weekend – and realised the paramedic would have seen them. Even so, I remained silent, not knowing how I should answer.

'Do you know a big fella, Magill?'

I laughed and met his eye.

'I love him. He's brilliant craic.'

'You work with him?'

I nodded.

'I work with his mother,' he said. 'She's the same!'

'I'd heard she was a paramedic.'

It was strange being inside an ambulance for the second time in five days. Half of me felt foolish, wishing I hadn't, for the second time, been such a drama queen. But the other half was worried. I hadn't imagined both my collapses, after all. I couldn't have a brain tumour, could I? This time, I thought, I won't leave the hospital without finding out what's wrong. I need a scan of my brain.

We arrived, and I was left with the triage nurse.

'What appears to be wrong tonight?' She gave me a glance that seemed to say, *I'm really busy and there is clearly nothing wrong with you.*

I repeated what I'd told the paramedics and she wrote it all down. Then, glancing at her watch, sighing, she told me to sit in the waiting area.

'You'll have a long wait,' she said. 'We're busy tonight.'

I repeated this to Diane, who was sitting in the waiting area.

'Does she think I've nowhere better to be on Easter Monday?'

'The nurse?' I nodded.

'I think she was in need of a tea-break.' I looked around. 'It doesn't look too busy, does it?'

'No. Talking of tea, do you want a cuppa?'

'Oh, yes, please.'

'Do you want some chocolate, too?'

I shook my head.

'I'm chocolated out. I ate the whole egg – the one you gave me. Thanks, by the way.' I stood up. 'I'm just going outside to ring Adrian.'

Stepping outside the entrance to A & E, I pressed the contact for Adrian and he answered on the first ring. I explained what had happened.

'It was just like before, at work,' I said. 'But I'm grand now.'

'Well, don't go home without getting an answer. And this time, don't accept a so-called diagnosis of "unexplained loss of consciousness".'

'Okay,' I said. 'I'd be happier with the "explained" kind.'

'I can come home,' he said. 'I can get a boat from Stranraer to Belfast tomorrow first thing. I'll be with you by lunchtime ... or by early afternoon anyway.'

I told him not to bother, that he should continue his final week of physiotherapy in Scotland. Then, feeling the night chill on my bare legs – I was still wearing shorts and flip-flops – I walked back into A & E. Diane handed me a paper cup and we sat, side by side, on plastic chairs, chatting, enjoying this rare time to talk without the interruptions of daily life. Diane is my only sibling and we've always been close, but usually, as the elder, I was the one looking after her.

The waiting area was quiet. A man with a shaved head sat, slumped, clearly the worse for drink or maybe drugs. A television sounded in the background. After an hour or so, Diane asked the receptionist on the desk how long the wait would be.

'Apparently they're tremendously busy,' she said, sitting down beside me. 'It'll be hours yet.'

Overhearing this, a young couple sitting next to us decided to give up, to go home and return the following day. I opted to stay.

Diane was busily texting when I shouted at her in panic, 'Diane it's happening again!' Suddenly my head felt filled with cotton wool, the waiting area started to spin and my stomach started to churn. I feared I might see the Easter egg I had eaten again but, as suddenly as the feeling had appeared, it disappeared.

'Are you okay? What on earth is wrong with you, I wonder?' said Diane.

I wondered the same. I wasn't imagining the feeling in my head. What was it? One minute I was completely fine, then suddenly I wasn't. I told myself it was nothing serious.

Time passed. It would be my turn soon, surely? Feeling my whole body fill with cotton wool again, I slid off the chair and lay flat on the floor. Maybe lying on a cold floor would make the feeling disappear.

'Di, please tell them to help me! There is something wrong in my head.' I felt terrified. There was something very wrong with me and no one believed it.

Diane ran off. I heard her asking for help. Then the triage nurse was standing over me, staring into my face.

'There is no need to cause a scene,' she said. 'If you wanted a bed you could have asked.' I wanted to scream at her.

Diane helped me to my feet and the nurse motioned for us to follow her through double doors. The feeling, although not entirely gone, was lifting from my head. *No wonder no one believes me*, I thought.

The nurse pointed at a trolley in the long corridor and said, 'Lie down.' Attaching me to a machine, she looked at it, then back at me. 'Everything is normal.' But how could everything be normal when I felt like this?

The nurse walked away without saying anything more. I wanted to know when I'd be seen by a doctor. Would a doctor scan my head? But I lay silently on the trolley. I didn't want to do anything that would make the feeling come back.

The long white corridor felt empty and cold. I began to shiver. An elderly man, restless on a bed in front of mine, kept trying to climb off. The nurse and what must have been his daughter chastised him in unison, telling him to stay on his trolley.

A neighbour, recognising Diane, came and asked us what we were doing there. I described what had happened and she said, 'Goodness, you don't think you're having a stroke, do you?'

'At my age?' I said. 'But I do feel really weird.'

'It's a nightmare, this place,' she said. 'I'm here with my mother. The poor thing. She's broken her hip. She's in dreadful pain.'

Later, Dad arrived with David. They had come to keep us company and to give us a lift home once we were ready. They had left Emily, Adam and Hannah in the care of my mother. I smiled. I might be a grown woman, a police officer, but I was still Daddy's little girl! I was grateful. Talking to them helped pass the time, at least.

At least six hours had crept by when, finally, I was taken into a cubicle. I repeated my story to the young doctor. He did all the usual checks, testing my reactions and asking me to follow his finger with my eyes. Then, asking me to stand up, he checked my balance. He asked me to lift my arms, then to touch my nose.

'You're fine,' he said. 'All your stats are normal. There's a haze behind one of your eyes. We'll schedule you for a CT scan. You will get a letter in the post telling you when.' Then he pronounced me fit to go home.

As I sat up on the hospital bed, listening to the young doctor, a tremendous feeling of death surged through me and filled my body. This was unlike the previous feeling. It was all encompassing. I was petrified.

'Will somebody please help me?!' I was yelling now, shouting out that I wasn't some madwoman – I was a police officer. 'I can see three clocks above me. I know, logically, there's just one. There is something wrong in my head. Somebody, please, help me!'

A nurse, shouting over me, said, 'Clodagh, what drugs have you taken?' Turning to my sister, and to my father and brother-in-law who had joined her, she shouted, 'What drugs is she on?'

'I'm *not* on drugs! I'm a police officer. I'm fucking *dying*.'

Time was running out and nobody was listening. I knew I had to say goodbye. I turned to Diane, standing at my bedside, and said, 'Bye Diane.' Turning to my father, I tried to spit out the words, 'Bye, Dad,' but I couldn't get them out.

Then everything came to a stop.

Fear left me. The room was full of bright white light. It was the same room I had been in, but everyone had disappeared. Where were they? Was I dead? Two people were standing beside me where Diane had been. I didn't know them. I could see them but I couldn't make out their features. Who were they? There was a warmth coming from them. I felt safe. My head was completely clear.

I didn't want to be dead – but it felt okay. In fact, it felt safe. These people would look after me.

And then my peace was shattered. I could hear Diane screaming horribly. Someone was slapping my face, hard.

'Clodagh, Clodagh! You can't die. Not now. You can't!'

Suddenly I felt pain, terror and confusion again. I could hear voices shouting. It was as if Diane had pulled me back into the room, back to life.

And that was when it happened. The seizure. For the briefest of moments I knew where I was. My head was clear and I was aware of everything that was going on. I could hear and see and think logically, but I couldn't control my body. It was writhing violently across the bed. I vomited over and over again. And the worst thing was I could hear the same nurse shouting, 'Clodagh, you need to stop this! You need to stop this, and tell us what drugs you're on.'

Furious, I wanted to scream that she was wrong. I hadn't taken any drugs. But the world went black.

That was the middle of Monday night. The next thing I knew, it was Wednesday morning.

CHAPTER SIX

The Stroke Ward

I have been in intensive care for nine days. Afternoon visiting is coming to an end. Adrian is about to go for dinner. Michelle, my favourite nurse, returns from her break. She introduces herself to Adrian and asks him how he met me.

He explains about the police and tells her what my usual duties are.

'Clodagh,' she says, 'you must be a fit young woman.'

'You are,' says Adrian. 'You run four miles a day, just for fun, and you're not happy unless you're faster than me.'

Looking at me, they smile. I feel included and understood. I feel like myself again, not a lifeless body in a bed, a person no one realises is there. Michelle starts splashing with a basin of water. Adrian takes that as his cue to leave and kisses me gently on the forehead.

Michelle places a damp cloth onto my forehead, then smooths lotion onto my arms. I'm starting to realise I haven't smelt anything since the stroke. I haven't smelt Adrian's aftershave. Diane and my mum always wear perfume and I haven't smelt anything when they've been close to me. I never smell the creams they apply after a bed-bath – and I know they would have a scent. I try to imagine the smell of the lotion.

Michelle talks to me like she has always known me.

'You've got a lovely smile, Clodagh,' she says, although I can't actually smile. 'Shall I clean your mouth and try to get rid of that fur?'

I can think of nothing better. I blink frantically: *yes, yes, yes*. Michelle gently cleans the inside of my mouth with the little sponge on a stick. I try to smile.

'You like this, don't you?'

It's absolute heaven! Nobody has touched the inside of my mouth since I arrived. When Diane wets my lips, I have no way to communicate to her that I'd like her to clean inside my mouth. I know from Adrian that I have an infection in my mouth. He says it is disgusting. I've had a surgical procedure, a tracheostomy. It is to help me breathe. The tubes have been removed from inside my mouth, but they've cut a hole in my neck and put a tube in there instead.

This worries me. If my doctors have decided to give me a tracheostomy, does this mean they think I will always be on a ventilator? All I know about my condition I've heard from Adrian. No one is telling me anything. It's worrying me. I want to ask questions. Is there something else wrong with me – something more than the stroke and the mouth infection? Will I ever be able to breathe on my own again? I thought that when the tubes were removed from my mouth I would be able to move my lips and tongue, to make some sound, at least. But nothing moves. My tongue is no longer sore but now my neck hurts.

'There is a spray – fake saliva. You can get it in different flavours. Do you want to try it?' Michelle asks. I blink once. She rushes off and returns with a little bottle. 'I knew we had some of this somewhere,' she says. 'It's banana flavour.'

She sprays into my mouth. It's like manna from heaven! I wonder who invented it. It is quite possibly the best invention ever! My mouth felt as dry as the Sahara. It's as if someone has opened a dam. I blink and blink to say, *I want more*.

An hour later, I'm still savouring the moisture in my mouth from the fake saliva when Dr Maguire appears beside my bed.

'Good afternoon, Clodagh. I'm Dr Gabriel Maguire,' he says in a soft southern-Irish accent. I like him. He talks directly to me; he doesn't treat me like an idiot. But I wish he'd stop telling me his name. I got it the first time we met. 'We're moving you out of intensive care – you're well enough for the stroke ward now.' I don't know what to think. Is this a good thing or a bad thing? Thirty-five years old and well enough for the stroke ward!

In truth, I was expecting to be moved at some point. I've overheard conversations during the past few days – should I be a neurology patient or a stroke-ward patient? I hope that life will be easier on the stroke ward. I might even get well enough to go to Fiona's wedding.

As the porters wheel me out of intensive care, I pray that the stroke ward will be full of nurses like Michelle. My bed clunks to a stop beside a window. There's not much of a view – I'm looking at another part of the hospital. The sun is shining in through it. It's even hotter here than intensive care. A nurse apologises to me because the fan is on.

'It's cold in here,' she says, and I hear the click of a button. She has turned it off.

Mum and Dad appear by my bedside. I'm crying. I know my mouth opens now. Whenever I yawn or cry my mouth opens wide. But I have no control of it, so when I actually want to move my mouth I can't, and I make no sound. Tears roll down my face. I'm so hot. I hate the tears – they sting my eyes and tickle my neck. My hair is too hot around the back of my head.

'What's wrong?' says my mum in a distressed voice. I want to scream, *Will someone just turn on the fan and wipe my eyes?*

Mum briefly disappears then reappears at my bedside with the same nurse who turned my fan off.

'What's wrong, Clodagh?' she asks in a concerned voice.

I read her name badge and think, *I'd love to answer you, Sarah, but how can I with nothing but blinks to work with?*

Sarah turns to my mother and tells her, 'It's the move from intensive care to the stroke ward that is upsetting her. She will soon settle.' I know from the tears building in my mums' eyes that she isn't convinced of it.

Mum is a quiet person. It's hard for her, I'm sure, to understand what has happened to me. How do you take in that the young, healthy daughter you are so proud of has had a stroke? She and my dad stay by my bed, looking helpless. I can't stop my silent cries. I'm suffering and I have no way to let anyone know.

I can't see now because my eyes are stinging terribly, but I feel a gentle kiss on my forehead. I hope it's Adrian. I hear my mum sob, 'I don't know what's wrong with her. The nurse doesn't know either.'

I feel a cold cloth wipe my eyes. It moves over my face, my neck, my chest. I can see again. It's Adrian. Immediately he's understood that I can't see. He asks, 'Are you too hot?'

I blink once. I am so relieved he is here. He knows to ask me closed questions.

'Do you want the fan on?'

Again, I blink once. If I could, I would squeal with happiness. I love him. I feel the cool air move over my body as the blades of the fan rotate. I can feel the sweat on my skin evaporate. Adrian positions a damp cloth on my forehead. It is ice cold. Relief. I feel my body relaxing. I try to smile at him.

'Your mum and dad have gone. They're upset after all that. I know this is awful for you, pet, but try to be patient with them.'

Their visits are always painful. They don't know what to say to me. They don't hug me and I can't hug them. How can I tell them about my day, when all I can do is lie here like a corpse? They can't bring me grapes or chocolate or fruit juice on their daily hospital visits, because I can't eat or drink. I want to reassure them, to tell them that I will be okay. Everything about this is wrong. And Adrian is telling me to be patient?

I want to ask him exactly what Dr Maguire says is wrong with me. Word for word. I wait for him to tell me, but he doesn't. This maddens me. I need to talk about the past week – and all that has happened. All anyone will tell me is that I've had a stroke. But which kind, and when I will get better? How long will I be in hospital? I *have* to hear the details!

'Do you think you could spell, Clodagh?' Adrian stares at my face.

I blink once. I knew Adrian would find a solution to my not being able to talk. I don't know what he is planning to do but I'm willing to try anything.

'I've been thinking – I could go to a hardware shop and buy a piece of clear Perspex. I could get a permanent marker and write the alphabet on the Perspex. Then I could add something like a ruler to act as a cursor. Basically, a transparent board that has all the letters of the alphabet on it. I could hold it up and look at your eyes. You could look at a letter, then I could write the letter down. You could spell words out to me; we could talk! I miss having a two-way conversation with you.'

I smile, and he kisses me. Then I blink three times.

'I love you too, Clodagh. You are going to beat this thing,' he says. 'I'll make that board for you and bring it tomorrow.'

Adrian knows how the heat distresses me. Before he goes home, he settles me for the night, making sure I'm comfortable and happy. He places a fresh cold cloth on my head, makes sure the cold air from the fan is hitting my body and leaves me covered with just a sheet. It's bliss. Sleeping is almost impossible when you can't adjust your position, but tonight I feel great. Tonight I just might sleep.

The night nurse arrives and I smile at her. My mouth sometimes makes a very small smile if I really try – even if no one realises that's what it is. I feel like I'm smiling, at least.

She doesn't smile back. Maybe my crooked smile doesn't look like a smile. She whips off my cold cloth and hangs it neatly on the radiator next to my bed. Briskly, she walks over to the other side of the bed and turns off the fan.

'It's freezing in here,' she says. 'What were the day nurses thinking? We'll have you dying of pneumonia!'

As she gives me my bed-bath, I try to catch her eye. I blink frantically at her whenever she does look at my face. I want to scream. I want to tell her that it's the heat that will kill me, not the cold. She's a stroke nurse. Adrian has found out about some of the after-effects of stroke. He's told me that the body's temperature control sometimes doesn't work. Doesn't she know this?

I can tell she is a perfectionist, though, as she gently washes my arms, my legs and every part of my body.

'We'll soon have you comfortable again,' she says. Taking my arms, she carefully folds them across my chest. Then she pulls the sheet up around my shoulders. Smiling, she looks at me, admiring her work. I want her to ask me if I'm comfortable. I want her to look at my eyes. I want her to realise that inside I'm screaming, *Please don't leave me lying like this all night!* She walks off and I hear her talk softly to the elderly patient next to me.

The tracheostomy hurts my throat dreadfully. I picture the wound in my neck around the inserted tube – swollen, angry and red. Sweat starts to leak from every pore in my body. I stare at the nurse, willing her to look my way. I look at the clock. I will be in this position for at least eight hours. Surely she will look at me. Surely she will notice my red face and sweat-soaked hair? The ward darkens. She has left.

I watch the clock. Adrian will make his nightly phone call at ten o'clock. I hear the ring of a telephone and, soon after, the nurse pops in and tells me that he's called. I pray hard that he's mentioned the fan to her, and the cold compress, but she says, 'I reassured him that you're comfortable and set for the night. I think he's happy now.' Then she leaves. I watch the back of her blue tunic disappear into the darkness of the corridor. I despair.

Earlier, I heard an auxiliary nurse compliment the staff nurse. She said, 'I wish I was as smart as you. You're a great nurse.'

Neither of you knows anything about nursing! I wanted to shout at them both. *You're great at reading machines, but how about actually observing patients? Adrian and Diane talk to me – so why can't you professionals do the same?*

I was hot in intensive care. The nights there were bad enough. But tonight I'm in danger of dying by overheating. I just know it. I stare at the clock, willing the hands to move, hoping I can hang on until morning. I force my eyes to stay open because I know that, if I sleep, I will never wake up.

It's just one night, I tell myself. Just eight hours. Eight hours isn't a long period of time. I have worked 12-hour shifts. Eight hours is a short one. Tomorrow Adrian will bring me his board and everything will be okay.

I must keep myself occupied or I'll go mad. The sweat on my body is making the air around me humid. I can't do anything physically to help myself – but there's nothing wrong with my mind, or my memory.

I need to think of some time in my life before all of this happened. I transport myself to Botswana. Adrian and I travelled there at the hottest time of the year. The heat was intense, but the wildlife is the most dramatic at that time.

I close my eyes tight. If I'm to survive tonight, I must believe I'm there. I remember floating in a dugout canoe with Adrian along the Chobe River. We set up camp in the Okavango Delta. The afternoon sun caused me to get sunburnt as we swam in the delta. We laughed as locals told us it was called 'a hippo-shit spa'.

At night we listened to the hippos bathing in the delta as we lay sweltering in our hot and airless tent. I lay there, wincing every time Adrian touched my sunburnt skin. I didn't die there – in that airless heat. This is just the same, I tell myself. It's no different.

But it *is* different. On holiday I could fan myself with my hands. I could wipe the sweat from my face. I could take a drink of water and, in the morning, wash the sweat off in the delta. I was in control. And now I'm not. That is the worst thing. The absolute helplessness. My neck is sore, the sweat is tickling the wound in my throat and there is absolutely nothing I can do.

I need to focus my mind. I turn to God. He didn't listen to me when I asked to die, but maybe he will listen when I ask to live. I've never needed him so much.

Please, God, I pray, *don't let me die. Keep me alive.* Then I wonder if I got his name wrong. Hedging my bets, I pray to every deity I can think of – Allah, Buddha, Jehovah. *Whoever you are, please help me! Keep me alive until morning!*

I don't know which one of them answers my prayer, but it is answered. I watch the sky lighten as dawn breaks, signalling the beginning of a day I thought I would never see. The corridors of the hospital start to fill with noise.

I've made it.

With the morning, and a bed-bath, comes relief. Heaven, for me, is a bowl full of water. My heart lifts. Today Adrian is coming in with the board and I will be able to spell. Then I can tell the nurses to keep me cool, to leave my fan on. I cling on to that thought. I just have to get to visiting time and Adrian will arrive.

But by the time Adrian arrives I'm in crisis again. Something is wrong. I can feel death all over me again. My body is tight and rigid. It's the way it was before the seizure hit. Before the stroke. Nobody took any notice of my distress back then, and they definitely won't now. The nurses are walking backwards and forwards, tending to patients. They pause at my bed, they smile, they say hello. They don't see the panic in my eyes. They don't realise I am dying and there is nothing I can do about it! Then I see Adrian. My eyes lock onto his.

He walks into the ward, directly to my bed, and says, 'Clodagh, is something wrong?'

I blink once for yes.

'Are you in pain?'

I blink once and he rushes to the nearest nurse and asks for painkillers. They feed them into the tube in my nose. But I'm not in pain. Not really. It's just that I can't think how else to explain that something *is* badly wrong – that I feel I'm dying – when all I can do is blink. I look for the board. Adrian hasn't given it to me yet. He must have it but his priority right now is to make sure I'm okay.

'You're still not right, are you?'

I blink twice: *no*, and hold his gaze, willing him to read my eyes, to read the message in them – *I'm dying.*

Adrian closes the curtains around my bed, shutting out the bustle of the ward. He fills a basin with water from the sink, checks the temperature and begins to sponge me. And he keeps on going, talking to me all the while. For hours he gently sponges my face, my chest, my arms and my legs. I know that he's saving my life. There is death all over me and he is washing it off. My body relaxes. I am alive because Adrian has done that.

I don't know how he knew what was needed, when I didn't even know it myself. But he knew. He has no medical training, yet he could sense it.

'You're okay now, aren't you?' he says.

I blink once.

'I could tell from your eyes,' he says, answering my silent question. 'I could see fear in them before. Real fear, as if you were on the edge of death.' He smiles. 'Now I just see you looking back at me!'

I stare at Adrian. I have never needed a man in my life before but now I do. I need Adrian, since nobody else seems to want to communicate with me. It seems like he's the only one who can keep me alive right now. I wait for him to show me the board he told me he was making. He chats about home, about people from work who are asking about me. He says his daughter Caoimhe was very upset when he told her I was ill.

'She can't wait to see you, Clodagh,' he says. 'Just as soon as you feel ready.' He chats to the nurse, who pops her head through the closed curtains, asking if my pain is better.

He settles me for the night. He turns on the fan and puts a cold, damp cloth on my forehead. It's getting time for him to leave, but he still hasn't mentioned the spelling board. He leans down to kiss me. I blink as fast as I can, hoping he may see the desperation I feel.

'What's wrong, Clodagh?' He looks puzzled, and then he understands. Grimacing, he says, 'Oh, the spelling board!'

I smile, blink once and wait for him to show me. He sits down again.

'I'm sorry. I know I said I'd bring it today, but I haven't made it yet. I did get the Perspex. It was so late when I got home yesterday, I just fell into bed. There was no time today. I'll make it tonight and bring it tomorrow. I promise.'

My heart sinks. Will I survive another night without it? I give him a dirty look – pleased it's one thing I seem to be capable of.

This is life or death! I tell him with my eyes. He looks guilty. He leaves, and I pray that a different night nurse will appear. Or, if it's the same one, that she will realise my need to be cool.

But God isn't listening tonight. Nor is Buddha, nor any of the others. I want to scream. The same nurse arrives into the ward, wheeling a large medicine trolley. She walks towards me and stops to examine a clipboard attached to the foot of my bed. She sighs as she moves around beside me. It's a nightmarish *déjà vu*. She whips the cold cloth off my forehead; she turns off the fan. She gives me my nightly bed-bath, then places my arms across my chest and pulls the sheet up to my shoulders.

I feel like a corpse in a coffin. When my grandmother died, there was an open coffin and her arms were placed across her chest, just as mine are now. I remember thinking it looked unnatural, that nobody would ever choose that position. She was so still. I must look like a corpse in a coffin with a gurgling pipe coming out of my neck! I feel as if I've been buried alive. I might as well be dead.

Panic sets in. I just can't do this for a second night. I'm so hot. The beads of sweat are little beads of torture as they roll slowly across my skin. The wound on my neck is throbbing. I cry. I try to make noise. Why can't I? Eventually, the nurse notices my tears and open mouth. Peering down at me she asks, 'What's wrong?'

This cannot be happening to me! I want to strangle her. Why can't she ask me a closed question – 'Are you in pain?' or 'Are you too hot?' How can I answer, 'What's wrong?'

'Oh, look,' she says, glancing at my monitor. 'Your heart rate has gone right up.' She feels my pulse, then orders an electrocardiogram.

I'm pleased. At least my heart is working. If I keep panicking will my heart beat faster? Then will I have the company of the nurse throughout the night? Maybe an ECG technician will know I can answer closed questions with blinks.

She arrives in a bustle and whips the sheet off me to attach the electrodes to my chest. The flow of air across my body is the best feeling in the world. I sigh in relief, but all too soon the electrodes are removed, the sheet replaced and tucked in around my neck.

'It's stress,' says the technician. 'Her heart is fine.'

The nurse nods.

'I thought as much. She's just moved from intensive care and seems to cry a lot. It often unsettles people when they arrive here to a more relaxed environment.' Turning to me, she smiles. 'You'll get used to this place.'

Get used to this place? I don't *want* to get used to this place. Neither of the women tries to communicate with me – not really. How stupid do you have to be to not see I'm too hot? I glare at the two women. Between them, they are going to kill me.

I close my eyes, I recall every detail from when I went skydiving in Namibia. It was so hot up in the aeroplane but, as the man attached to my back hurled the two of us out of the plane, I felt euphoric. My cheeks were flapping from the speed we were falling at; the purple skydiving suit was flapping on my arms and legs. Surrounded by gushing air, I laughed and laughed. Then the parachute opened. The air became warmer as we gradually floated to the ground. I felt so free. The white sands of the desert were below me. I could see sharp lines where it met the sea.

I feel peaceful as I recall it. But when I open my eyes, the reality of my paralysed body hits me all the harder. I can't move. There's no air, just a stultifying warm stillness. I cry, and the tears roll down behind my ears.

Adrian promised he would make a board for me to spell with. He swore he would make it and bring it tomorrow. I really can't do one more night without it. This has to be the last night I battle to live. Without that promise, I swear, I would give up the struggle right now. It's too hard.

I can't do it any more.

CHAPTER SEVEN

The Spelling Board

I've never been able to sit still – it's just not me. I thought that the minute I was out of danger and safely in the stroke ward, my rehabilitation would begin. And that would mean action. But nothing has happened yet. And the nursing is less intensive here, so the nurses aren't around me as much. There is more activity in the stroke ward, more hospital staff. It's all bustle. But when you can't talk and can't move, people forget that you are there. It sounds crazy. I am never alone, but I have never felt so isolated.

When will I be able to talk? I pray that it's soon. I'd go mad if it weren't for Adrian. Since that first day, when he realised I could blink, he has done everything in his power to help me. And the first thing he did was to ask the nurses in intensive care for help.

'Could you give Clodagh some cards to help her communicate what she needs?'

The nurse looked blank.

'She could blink at the right one,' he said. 'They would allow her to communicate, "I'm in pain," or "My mouth is dry."'

'Oh, cue cards!' the nurse said.

'Is that what they're called? Yes, something to allow her to communicate.'

'We don't use those in here,' she said as she checked my chart. 'Not in intensive care. It's too early. The speech-and-language department will visit Clodagh once she moves to the stroke ward and assess her abilities.'

The moment I arrived on the stroke ward, Adrian asked again. And he was told that someone from speech-and-language therapy would visit me soon. He was fuming.

'I don't know why no one will help us,' he said. 'I want to be able to talk to you now, not whenever the *hospital* decides the time is right.'

That's why he has decided to make me a spelling board. And today, at last, I will have it! Adrian has promised. I'm thinking about this when a petite woman arrives on the ward and approaches my bed.

'Clodagh Dunlop?' She checks the name on my chart. 'I'm Sarah-Jane. I'm from speech and language.'

At last! But who is this woman? Sarah-Jane has long, dark-blonde hair pulled back into a low pony tail. I can tell she is stylish because, unlike all other medical staff, she is not wearing trainers, but a nice pair of brown brogues. I stare at her eyes. *I'm strong*, they say. *I know my job.* I feel somewhat reassured.

There's an older woman with her. The older woman begins to do a series of tests with me.

'Stick out your tongue,' she says. I try, but I can't. 'Puff up your cheeks.' I try, but I can't. 'Can you lick your teeth?' I try, but nothing in my mouth moves. Why can't I move my tongue? This is bizarre! What type of stroke is this? I feel that Sarah-Jane is training the older woman from the way she's keeping a watchful eye on her and I feel resentful. I'm being used as a guinea pig.

Sarah-Jane moves over. I can tell she is frustrated by the woman's ability. She looks at me and takes over.

'Clodagh, this is an electronic Eyegaze spell board. It's a communication device that lets the user opposite you track your eye movements. It will help you spell out whatever you want to say. You're the first person in this hospital to use it. Shall we give it a try?'

She holds up a black rectangular tablet and looks at me through a hole in the centre of it.

'Now, as you see, there are six differently coloured blocks around the outside of the spelling board. Inside each coloured block are six coloured letters or numbers. If you want to select a letter, look at the one you want and blink. Then look at the block with the same colour as that letter and blink again.'

My mind is racing. This sounds complicated. Will I be able to use it?

As if sensing my fears, Sarah-Jane continues, 'The letter c is in the blue block. If you want to select the letter c, you look at the blue block and blink. The letter c is coloured white, so to fully select it you have to look at the white block and blink. Two blinks for every letter, okay? And the letters you've selected will appear on the screen at the bottom here. Do you want to try?'

I blink once. I understand how it works. The relief that I will be able to spell out what I want to say makes me feel like I could burst with happiness. I want to tell Sarah-Jane she may have saved my life by bringing this spelling board to me. I imagine myself jumping from my bed and hugging her tightly, yelling, 'Thank you, thank you!'

'That's great. The nurses were telling me you have a boyfriend called Adrian. Can you spell Adrian, Clodagh?' She holds up the board.

Of course I can! I'm not stupid. I am excited to begin. I start, but it's hard to do with only my eyes. If only my head moved a little. I look at each letter, within its block. Blinking at the letters I want to select is tedious, slow and physically demanding. I'm exhausted when I finish. I've spelt out 'Adiav'. What's wrong with me?

Sarah-Jane decides to ignore my mistake.

'Well done,' she says. 'That's really great. I'll leave the board here. You can show it to your friends and family over the weekend. You can tell them how to use it.' And, promising me she would be back early next week, both she and the older woman walk away.

I watch her as she leaves, her long pony tail moving across the back of her white tunic. And I curse her for not thinking the thing through. It's crazy, I think, when you can't communicate in any way, how everyone treats you so very differently from when you can. I have no expression; I'm making no sound. There's no way for anyone to tell what I'm thinking – so they just assume I'm happy.

But she knows I can't talk; she knows I can't move. She must be aware that, without speech and movement, I can as little explain a spelling board to someone else as travel to the moon. And she has left it on my locker. What if no one notices it? Well, it doesn't matter. Adrian is bringing the board he has made.

Later, when Adrian strides into the ward, he is carrying a large object under his arm in a black binbag. He must have his board. Brilliant. I can't wait to start spelling things out to him. We have so much to do in such a short period of time. I need him to make a lot of signs for me. Surely, if I have signs, the night nurses will stop trying to kill me!

Adrian leans down and kisses me on the forehead. When he stands up his eyes slide to my locker and he notices the official board.

'Oh, speech and language have been here, have they?'

I blink: *yes.*

'About time.' He picks up the hospital board and tries to work out how to use it. It doesn't take him long. He's a typical police officer – naturally inquisitive and good at solving problems. He lets nothing beat him. 'This is great!' he says. 'Really high tech. Let's give this a try.'

I don't want to use the official board. I hate technology – Adrian knows that. And if we can't work it, will I get my signs? I want to use his version. I don't want to waste any more time. I glare at Adrian, hoping he can read what my eyes are saying. *Hurry up! This isn't a new toy to mess about with! This is life or death for me!*

I have no choice but to try, though, as Adrian holds up the official spelling board and watches my eyes. I select each letter I want. It is frustratingly slow. I spell out, 'Will you make me signs?' Adrian looks at the spelling board to read what I have spelt out. He looks puzzled. My chest tightens.

'I think I got it wrong. Let's try again.'

I spell again: 'Will you make me signs?' Adrian deliberately and slowly reads what I have spelt out but shakes his head. Is he an idiot? Why can't he understand what he is reading aloud: 'Will you make me signs?'

This isn't working. It *has* to, or I might not survive. I hate him so much right now. I cry. I wish I could make a sound. If I could, I would scream at him right now for being so stupid.

'It's okay,' he says. 'We've got time. I'm staying here until I understand what you want.'

We try again. I spell out something different. Adrian stares at the spelling board and says slowly, 'They are trying to kill me.' He looks at me. I blink once. He holds up the board to continue. He reads what I spell.

'You want me to make some signs?'

I blink once. He frowns in confusion.

'What for?'

I spell out: 'Above my bed.'

'What? You *can't* have signs above your bed.' He looks around the ward, indicating the bare walls. 'They'll never allow it!'

He stands there, staring at me. I can see disbelief in his eyes. It's the first time we've properly communicated in weeks and we are having a domestic. I panic. I need him to make the signs tonight or I will die.

I spell out: 'Please make me fucking signs or I will die.' I need him to understand how important this is. Without sound, without movement, all I have is language. I *have* to get across how important this is.

Adrian is starting to understand. I expand. I get too hot at night and I'm worried I might die by overheating. I spell out that the fan gets turned off at night. He nods. Finally. This is working! It's slow, yes. It's frustrating, definitely. But we are having an actual conversation!

Adrian makes his way to the nurses' station and returns with a marker and some white A4 paper. We spend the entire two-hour visiting time making signs. I spell out what I want him to put on each sign. Adrian writes each instruction in large writing on the paper and sticks it on the wall above my bed. *Do not turn fan off*; *Do not remove cloth from head*; *Leave arms by side*; *Do not cover arms with sheet*; *Spray mouth with fake saliva*.

As Adrian kisses me on the forehead to leave, I blink frantically.

'You want to spell something else?' he asks. Adrian holds the spelling board and watches my eyes as I blink at each letter I want. When I indicate that I'm finished he reads aloud what I've spelt out.

'Thank you, you rock. I love you.'

Adrian laughs and says, 'You are still a pain. Get some sleep. Love you too.'

The cloth stays on my head, the fan stays on, my arms are placed at my side and I'm not covered with a sheet. I fall into a deep sleep.

It's Saturday morning, I am buzzing that my signs have worked. A nurse stares into my face and introduces herself as Sarah from the Philippines. She smiles and tells me I'm beautiful.

'Clodagh, you're like Sandra Bullock,' she says.

I look into the eyes of Sarah number 2.

I don't believe you, my eyes tell her. I am very sure I'm not beautiful right now. But a part of me is reassured by what she says. I haven't seen my face in a mirror since the stroke, which must be three weeks ago. Diane has told me I have a crooked smile and I'm scared my face has changed.

Sarah starts to give me my morning bed-bath. A bed-bath is a very basic body clean, but Sarah takes her time and acts as if she is my own personal beautician. She shaves my underarms and legs and smooths on lotion afterwards.

'I can wash your hair. Would you like that?'

I blink once.

She massages my scalp, rinses off the shampoo and gently brushes my hair. All the time she talks to me in a gentle, reassuring way. I close my eyes tight. Sarah is so attentive that I can almost imagine I'm in a spa.

When she starts to clean my teeth, I'm positively euphoric. It's not easy for nurses to do more than swab around my mouth, because I can't spit or swallow, but Sarah has located a suction toothbrush that cleans my teeth and sucks out excess paste and water at the same time. And all the while, she tells me what perfect teeth I have.

'You're going to get well, beautiful Clodagh. I know it!' Sarah says. She sings to me and tells me she will pray for me too. She is a nurse sent from heaven! I love her. She doesn't use my new spelling board – I don't think she's noticed it – but it doesn't matter. She asks me closed questions I can answer with a blink or two, and she makes me feel like a fully functioning woman.

Later that day, when Adrian arrives for visiting, I feel happier and more relaxed than I have at any time since the stroke. I'm looking forward to telling him this with the spelling board. But when he picks it up, it doesn't work.

'I don't believe it!' His face looks furious. 'They've just got you this thing and already it's out of power.' I can hear the Sergeant Simpson tone entering his voice.

Sarah arrives at that moment, approaching my bed with a smile. Before she can tell Adrian about our day, he immediately attacks.

'Where is the charger for this?'

'I'm sorry,' she says, smiling, looking at the spelling board with interest. 'I don't know where it is.'

'What help is that?' Adrian glares at Sarah. 'Did you use the spelling board today?'

She shakes her head. Her eyes look at the floor.

Adrian is about to explode.

'That means you didn't care for Clodagh properly. You couldn't have.'

I hate this! I want to interrupt. I want to shout that Sarah has been wonderful. I watch, completely helpless to intervene. Waving the spelling board, Adrian continues his rant.

'This is how Clodagh communicates,' he says. 'I want to talk to her right now – I need to – and I can't. You need to go and get the charger now!'

I look at Sarah as she hurries away like a frightened rabbit. I try to catch Adrian's eye but he's too angry to look at me. He paces around the ward as he waits for her to return. He's still in a state of fury when a junior doctor appears and promises to contact speech and language on Monday.

'I'll make sure they bring the charger,' she says.

Staring the doctor down, Adrian loses it.

'Monday?' His voice is so loud that everyone in the ward is watching the scene. 'That's not good enough! How am I supposed to talk to Clodagh until then? Have you any idea what it's like for her? She can't talk or tell anyone how she feels. Do you realise this board changes all that?'

The young doctor opens and closes her mouth as if trying to find the right words, but Adrian isn't expecting an answer. He sighs dramatically and flings the board down on the bed.

'I have a meeting with Clodagh's consultant on Monday, and if you don't get a charger from somewhere, and get one now, I'll be telling your boss that Clodagh's levels of care are unacceptable.'

I feel sorry for the doctor as well now. She's so young, and she has been lovely to me. Maybe he has a point, but this wouldn't be happening if I could just talk. I hate not being able to talk and I hate him bawling Sarah out when she's been so wonderful.

Twenty minutes later, while Adrian is still sounding off about my care, Sarah appears, holding out a charger. Thanking her, if rather abruptly, Adrian plugs in the spelling board and makes it ready for use.

'I knew they would find one if they bothered to look,' he says, holding it up for me.

Moving my eyes to each of the letters, I spell out: 'I love Sarah. She is fabulous. Say sorry to her.' I give him a dirty look to emphasise my words.

Adrian laughs, 'You're still bossy, Clodagh.' He calls Sarah over, says sorry and repeats my praise. Sarah says she understands. She accepts his apology with good grace, as I suspected she would. When she has told Adrian what a beautiful person I am, making him smile, she leaves us alone together.

Now I have a way to communicate, I ask Adrian to tell me every detail about my illness. He answers every question I ask. But I know him. I know by his face that he isn't telling me everything.

Sunday passes peacefully, but on Monday night the nurse I don't like comes on duty and I tense up. She doesn't look at me. Shivering, she raises her hand to turn off the fan, just as she always does. Then her eyes flick to the signs above my bed and her hand stops.

Her gaze stays fixed above my head and I know she is reading my signs. She looks down at me, then back at the signs. Frowning, she looks at my face. I'm scared she'll ignore my instructions. As she gives me my bed-bath she glances at the signs now and then, taking them in. Then she looks at me, smiles, and follows each request to the letter. She reads the signs aloud to me when she is finished and confirms that each one is correct.

I've been unfair. This nurse wasn't trying to kill me for the past few nights – she was only doing what she thought was best. The spelling board has miraculously changed my world. I still don't sleep well – I'm uncomfortable and restless. But at least the fear of death has gone.

When Sarah-Jane from speech and language returns, she laughs.

'Look at your signs! You did this?' Still laughing, she pats my arm. 'Good girl! I'm impressed.'

We discuss the treatment to come, having a real conversation on the spelling board, and she treats me as a person – someone who understands everything she's telling me. She's become my ally. From then on I love her visits and work as hard as I can – not just because I want to get better, but also because I want to prove myself to her.

I think back to when I first saw her – how I thought she couldn't possibly be good at her job – and I realise how I misjudged her. She is superb at her job. I've been much too harsh on everyone caring for me. If only I could talk, everything would be different.

'We need to explore removing the tube and the surgical opening in your throat,' she says one day. 'Before it is removed, we need to wean you off the ventilation. You will have to breathe by yourself. I'm going to talk to the doctors and suggest we start the process.'

She checks that I am happy with this. I give one blink and she understands. Two days later, she arrives at my bedside with a smile on her face.

'Today we'll start the process of getting rid of that thing,' she says, pointing to the tracheostomy tube. 'I'm going to let the cuff down for a short time and see how you get on.'

I don't know whether to be pleased or terrified. It occurs to me that maybe the tracheostomy is why I can't talk. I'd do anything if it meant I could talk again.

I feel safe with Sarah-Jane. I trust her fully. She communicates with me as though I were able to chatter to her like I would have before stroke. When the cuff is first let down I feel anxious, but I stare into her eyes. She is watching me back, telling me to breathe, asking if I'm okay. I'm surprised when I manage to take some small breaths. This is wonderful. I can breathe. It's a struggle, but I can breathe! I take shallow breaths and tell myself to stay calm. *Breathe, just breathe.*

Over the next few days I breathe for longer. Half an hour, then an hour, and finally all day. It's still not easy. But, I tell myself, I need to think like an athlete. I realise my lungs need time to adjust, to get strong again. Keeping my struggles to myself, I just work with it.

Sarah-Jane appears as delighted as I am when it is agreed I can have the tracheostomy tube removed.

'That's good, Clodagh,' she says. 'Next we'll do a swallow test to try and get that tube removed from your nose.'

A swallow test? I'm disappointed. I thought that when the tracheostomy tube was removed I would be able to eat and drink. Just how helpless am I? Me, a health freak who loves fitness and worry about nutrition to feed my body. Why can't I just swallow? Why can't I just talk? It seems so bizarre. I can't be silent for the rest of my life!

Getting the tracheostomy tube removed is a weird sensation. They simply take it out of my throat and put a bandage on it. They say it will close over and heal of its own accord.

Next comes the day of my swallow test. Equipment is wheeled in on a trolley. I'm propped up into a seated position in my bed. Sarah-Jane tells me I'm having a procedure called a nasoendoscopy and that it might be uncomfortable but it won't hurt. She shows me a long, thin, flexible tube.

'It has a light and a camera at the end, so that we can look into your throat as you swallow. Okay?'

I blink once.

A technician with blue latex gloves approaches me and inserts the tube into my nose. I feel it move as it pushes further in. I expect it to make me cough or retch, but it does neither. There is no pain; its not uncomfortable.

Sarah-Jane steps beside me. I look at her. I feel reassured by her presence. I trust her. Sarah-Jane holds what appears to be a yogurt pot.

'This is a thickened fluid. It's apple flavour. I'm going to place a small amount in your mouth. You try to swallow it.'

I feel the coolness on my tongue as the thickened liquid is placed into my mouth on a small spoon. I'm getting the taste of apples, but it feels so heavy on my tongue. I want to let the liquid sit on my tongue, to savour the moment – I haven't had food in weeks – but I know that I must swallow what's in my mouth. I try. I watch the small screen in front of my bed and notice that my tongue is barely moving.

'Keep trying, Clodagh,' Sarah-Jane says. 'You can do it. I know you can!' It takes what feels like an eternity, but I manage to swallow. Everyone gathered around is saying well done. It reminds me of a parent cheering on a baby when it starts on solid food.

'Try another one.'

I do, and it isn't any easier the second time. Why can't I move my tongue or cheeks? Why can't I swallow? I just want to gulp down a glass of water. Will I ever be able to do that again? When am I going to be able to talk?

'You've got to retrain your mouth muscles,' Sarah-Jane explains. She spends time with Adrian, explaining how he can play a role in helping me do this. She encourages him to use an electric toothbrush to stimulate my tongue and my cheeks and instructs him to bring me thick, cold fruit smoothies. She talks about using special spoons covered in chocolate spread to encourage my tongue to move.

If I had to choose between talking or moving, I think to myself, *I would choose talking every time.* The thought of never making a sound again is terrifying. You are so vulnerable when you can't talk or communicate.

'It's funny,' Adrian says, as he patiently spoon-feeds me smoothies during visiting time, 'but in a weird way this feels like when we started running together.'

He laughs, but I know what he means. We're working together on something, just as we are when we're running. But, instead of aiming for better fitness, we're working towards getting me talking again. When the tracheostomy tube was removed, I was devastated. I was convinced that I'd be able to talk immediately but in fact I couldn't make a sound. I'm beginning to realise that, if I want to talk again, I am going to have to work harder than I ever have before.

For all that, I'm grateful to Sarah-Jane for insisting that the tube should come out. From conversations I overheard, I got the feeling that others thought it was too soon. Sarah-Jane has stuck her neck out for me and I won't forget it. She is the one person in the medical team who understands my burning desire to talk. She knows I will work as hard and as long as it takes and that Adrian will do whatever he can to help me.

On duty, before my stroke.

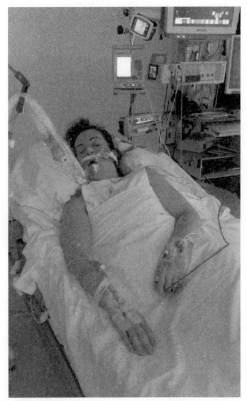

Waking to a nightmare – intensive care.

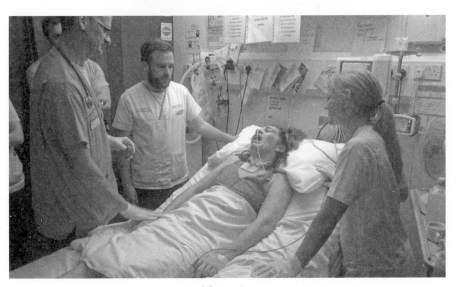

Silent cries.

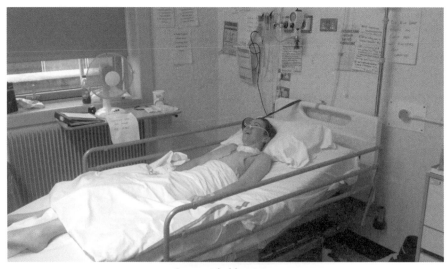

Surrounded by signs.

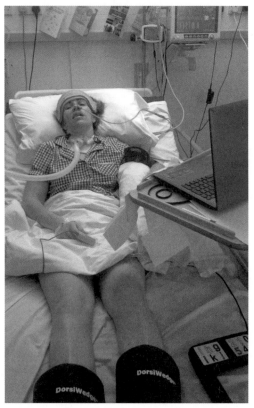

'Don't take the cold compress off my head!'

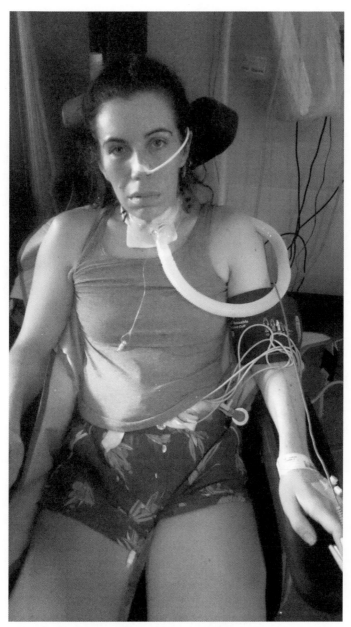

I'm a pyjama woman!

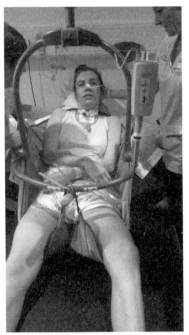

The hoist – I feel like I'm at Barry's
amusements in Portrush!

An afternoon of laughter
with KD.

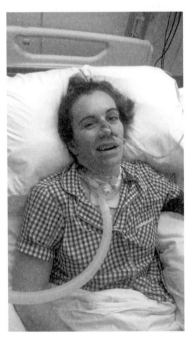

I try to smile but I don't know if I can.

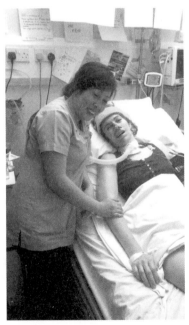

Sarah says, 'Clodagh, you're like
Sandra Bullock.'

I don't recognise myself.

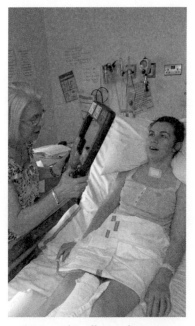

Mum and I talk together using
the spelling board.

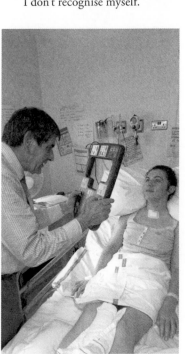

Dad and I use the spelling board.

My last night in the Royal and my
first Facebook post.

My thirty-sixth birthday.

A rare instance when Diane's and Adrian's visits coincide.

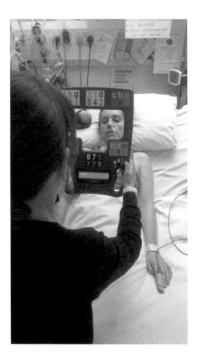

The spelling board allows me to talk to KD.

Diane and Fiona give me 'illegal' showers.

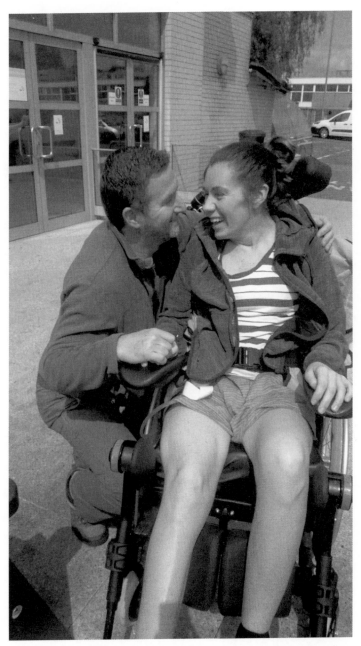

When Adrian visits I wheel myself out of the unit. We like the garden.

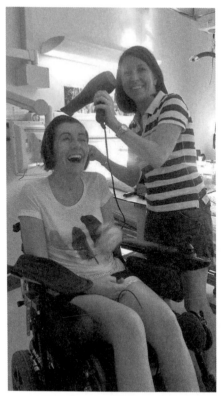

Diane gets me ready for date night
with Adrian.

I look like myself again – I escape to
the cinema.

I can lift a tumbler to my
mouth and drink with a straw.

I read everything I can
about stroke.

I soon learn the routine in rehab, including daily therapy.

No more hoisting! I'm happy I can use the Stedy.

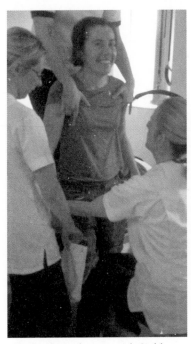

Daily physiotherapy with Siobhan.

I'm alive! I want to see the sea.

I need to get some sticks of rock …
nothing is impossible.

'Are you nervous?' 'No, I'm alive!' Mesmerised by the scenery.

Adrian hooks an adapted trolley onto the front of my wheelchair. We talk and even laugh.

Adrian and I spread our wings. We plan trips away. Sometimes we have to bring the wheelchair.

I can't stop smiling when I sit on my trike.

I've passed my test – I can drive an adapted car.

I've bought myself a brown leather briefcase.

CHAPTER EIGHT

Frustration and Fear

Every day, when Adrian has finished spoon-feeding me, we get out the spelling board and talk. This strange world – where I wear adult nappies, I'm spoon-fed and I spell out my conversations – almost seems normal to us now. Except it's not, of course. Normal life is still going on as well.

I spell out questions about work to Adrian. Is someone attending to my paperwork? Has anyone seen to bailers returning for interview at the station? Do my colleagues know I'm not faking this strange illness? I feel almost lazy, lying all day every day in bed, not changing position. What about our household bills? I'm quite sure the electricity company, the oil company and the mortgage lenders aren't interested in what's happened to me.

Adrian assures me that I don't have to worry about work and that, yes, that he is attending to the bills. He shows me pictures of the garden at our Forever House. The daffodils and cherry trees have come into bloom. It looks so pretty. I cry. Diane's children helped me to plant the daffodil bulbs. Adrian, as if sensing what I'm thinking, says, 'You'll be home soon enough. Stop worrying – you will beat this.'

The spelling board is magic! I can articulate my concerns and fears to Adrian about everything. The fact that I can't make a sound no longer matters in the same way. I still desperately want to talk, of course, but the spelling board means I have more control over my care.

Some nurses use the spelling board with me; others don't. But they all make a point of checking my care with Adrian. He teases me.

'You're practically in charge of this place,' he says. 'And for someone who can't move or talk, that's pretty good going, Clodagh!'

I feel safer now that I can communicate. At least, I usually do. But tonight, two nurses I haven't met before come on duty. One of them is a tall male nurse. As he walks around the ward, my fear builds. Is *he* going to give me my bed-bath? I don't want a man stripping me, washing my naked body and changing my nappy! I won't be able to bear it! When he approaches my bed, bringing the bowl of water, closing the curtains, I scream, *No!*

But, of course, I make no sound. I feel his hands on me. He is talking to me but I can't hear what he is saying. *He's just doing his job,* I tell myself over and over, but seeing his large hand on my white nappy – knowing he's about to whip it off and see the parts of my body that no man but Adrian should see – I cry.

Looking alarmed, he calls the other nurse over and she asks me what's wrong. She doesn't use the spelling board, so I can't answer her. Instead of asking questions, she grimaces and says, 'Just ignore her. I've heard that she always cries. It doesn't mean anything.'

My heart is breaking in sadness that I have become so helpless. Inside I'm screaming at him: *Please stop!* I shut my eyes to block out his hands on my body, but I can still feel them. I can't block out touch. I hear nervousness in his voice as he talks to me, but right now I don't care if he's kind. I just want my nakedness covered and for him to stop touching me. I feel the tug of my catheter and feel him wash the intimate parts of my body. *Please make this end!*

It does end. I hear the whoosh of the curtains opening. My nurse has concern in his voice.

'Are you sure she's okay?'

'She's fine,' replies the female nurse.

At work I have dealt with sexual crimes. I've always felt that they are horrific but thought if someone tried to hurt me I'd put up a good fight. Yet here I am, lying defenceless, a man touching me where I don't want him to. It makes me realise, again, how vulnerable I am.

I lie in bed and can't stop thinking that I'm helpless in the face of everything around me. The thought goes around and around in my head. Every footstep I hear in the night, every voice, I think, *They could hurt me and there is nothing I can do. I can't scream; I can't fight anyone off. I'd have to just lie here and wait for them to stop!*

I've heard reports on the news of vulnerable people being abused, physically and sexually, in care homes. That could happen to me here. Why not? There's nothing to stop it. I have had a stroke. I'm at the mercy of everyone around me.

I daren't go to sleep.

I count the minutes throughout the night, and the hours in the day, waiting for the moment when Adrian will visit. The minute he walks through the door and picks up the board, I spell out, 'I need a new sign. No fucking male nurses!'

Adrian looks uncomfortable. So, slowly and laboriously, I tell him what happened the night before. He is annoyed.

'I'll go find the sister and tell her what happened. It shouldn't have happened.'

It was just a job to the male nurse – I knew that – but to me it was terrifying and it felt wrong. I can't understand how a male nurse was allowed to touch intimate parts of my body, unaccompanied and with curtains drawn around us. Just me and him, alone. I feel violated. I want no more bed-baths from male nurses.

Adrian visits the nurses' station. He explains about my job – how I regularly deal with violent males. And how vulnerable I felt being washed by a man.

Adrian returns with two older female nurses. I can imagine him telling them, 'You need to come and speak to her.'

'This man of yours says we have to take extra care of you tonight.' They both look at me and smile. And just from the way they look at me, I know they will.

When they leave, I spell, 'Thank you, you're a star.'

Adrian leans over and kisses me on the forehead.

'Go easy on them, Clodagh. They're doing their best. We all are. You need to be patient.'

'I know. Change the subject.' I spelt. Adrian is still handsome, but I notice he's looking older these days. I wish he could lie down beside me. I wish I could hug him. I wish all this wasn't happening.

The next night, Adrian arrives at visiting and it's his turn to unburden himself. He tells me how alone he feels – how much he misses me in the Forever House.

'You've no idea how empty the house feels,' he says. 'I arrive home in the dark and nothing has moved. It's not like when we're on different shifts, because then there are always signs that you've been there. I can't stand it.'

I'm torn between anger, envy and empathy. How can he find this difficult when he can move and eat and speak? I'd do anything to be at home, but I listen intently. I have to, because he doesn't lift the spelling board and I know he doesn't want me to talk. He needs someone to listen right now. I worry about him.

He looks so sad, and there is nothing I can do to make things better.

Half the time, he explains, he doesn't go home at all.

'I can't bear to,' he says. Instead, he wanders down the road to the local pub for a drink. 'But that's not great,' he says, 'Because there's nobody there that I can confide in. I sit there surrounded by people, and we talk, but in my head I'm still alone.'

It seems he's drinking every day now. He has started smoking again too. He gave up for the two years we've been together. I worry I'm damaging his health.

He says he's thinking of asking KD and her husband Kris for dinner after they've visited me on Friday. 'It'll be good to have some company in the house,' he says.

I feel a little jealous. I've loved the nights we've spent with KD and Kris. But really I think it's a great idea.

The following night, when Adrian arrives, he's in a fury.

'I don't want to slag off your family, Clodagh. I know they love you and mean well.'

I wonder what's coming next.

'I mentioned to your mum that I've asked KD and Kris to dinner, and that they are staying the night, and she said, "Yes, that's okay. I give you my permission." I mean, what the hell?' He throws his hands up in a gesture of despair. 'I was speechless! I just looked at her, then I said, "They are staying with me. I have invited them. It's our home."'

It's my turn to be furious. Adrian really needs to cut my mum slack and stop being so sensitive. Haven't I got enough to deal with?

The next time Mum visits, she is fretting.

'I know Adrian is cross with me, but I didn't mean to make him upset,' she says. 'I was worried he would think I would be annoyed with the thought of him having KD and Kris in the house without you, and I wanted to reassure him that I wasn't. He just took me up wrong.'

My parents have given me everything. Things they never had. They gave me a good education. They made sure I went to grammar school, and to university. It wasn't easy for them. They set up the shop when I was in grammar school; before that Mum was a dinner lady. She cleaned people's houses, all to give Diane and me extra. She took me on the back of her bicycle to drama classes, to gymnastics. I had piano lessons too. Seeing me now must break her heart. I love her.

Visiting time each day brings with it a new story. I lie watching the clock, waiting for it. It's my favourite part of any day. One day, Adrian comes in, looking cheerful. He's visited a local clergyman. I'm surprised, because Adrian is not religious.

'Did he help?' I ask.

'He was great! He listened. I told him everything. How sad I am, how lonely it is … and it's helped. It really has.'

I'm pleased for him, and intrigued. I'm always telling Adrian he's a heathen.

'It was interesting,' he says. 'He asked me about God. He said, "Do you blame God for this?"'

'And do you?' I spell.

'No! Not at all. It's just that shit happens. I said that to the clergyman, and he laughed and said, "Well, that's a good start."' Adrian's quiet for a while. 'I hadn't expected it, but it was really pretty good.'

Every day is like *Groundhog Day*. Wake up. Morning bed-bath. Spoon-fed porridge. Stare at ceiling for hours. Spoon-fed flavourless puréed lunch. Visiting time. Stare at ceiling some more. Spoon-fed flavourless puréed dinner. Visiting time. Night bed-bath. Try to sleep. Stare at ceiling in darkness. Begin again.

I know all the nurses. But one day a new nurse bounces beside my bed.

'Hi! I'm Kerry, and I'm looking after you today,' she says, sounding much too perky for my liking.

She's young, with a girl-next-door face. She looks too keen for someone who's just started a shift. She's irritating me already. Kerry picks up the spelling board and begins to ask me lots of questions. Does she not know this is the time of the day I spend staring at the ceiling? I respond to her questions with polite – but short – answers.

But I find myself starting to warm to Kerry despite myself. She doesn't give up – she's determined to have a conversation with me. I like determined people who don't give up at the first hurdle.

When I'm moved out of the ward to a side-room of my own Kerry steals the position of my favourite nurse. When she's on duty she pops in as soon as she arrives on the ward, and when she spoon-feeds me porridge she acts as if it's an entirely normal thing to do.

Using the spelling board with speed and confidence, she drinks in the details of my life. She's fascinated by my job as a police officer, my life with Adrian and my travels. When she is my nurse for the day she makes a point of spending time with me. I can hear her voice in the corridor throughout her shift. It's not just me, of course. She makes a point of spending time with all her patients. She really is a special person.

Kerry is the first person to realise that I spend all day staring at the ceiling. When she selects *Marley & Me* for me to watch on the new laptop my work colleagues have bought me, I cry throughout the entire movie. I've never met someone so thoughtful and kind.

I love Sarah from the Philippines too. Where Kerry is lively and perky, Sarah is calm and gentle. When Sarah's on duty I know my teeth will be cleaned. And I love the way she tells me, just like Adrian, that I will get better for sure. It doesn't matter that she doesn't understand how to use the spelling board.

That is, it usually doesn't. But during one night when Sarah is on duty, I have a terrible pain where the catheter tube leaves my body. I blink frantically at

Sarah to tell her that something is wrong.

She picks up the spelling board, but can't work out how to use it. She's not alone in this. It's new and people are terrified of it. And there's no one she can ask.

'I'm sorry, Clodagh,' she says, staring at the board in frustration. 'I'm stupid with things like this.' She puts it down and starts pointing to different parts of my body. I blink twice as she points to my head, my mouth, my arms and legs. Then she sighs. She is looking like she just might cry. But then, with a determined look, she picks up her nemesis and says, 'I'm going to figure this out.'

Poor Sarah! She tries so hard, but doesn't understand it at all. She stares at my eyes, trying to establish what my blinks mean. She presses buttons. Random letters that make no sense together are appearing on the board.

Adrian has told me I need to be patient and I am. Sarah is patient too and, after an hour, a miracle happens. I've managed to spell out 'Cat'.

'Catheter!' she shouts. I blink: *yes*. She laughs with relief. I can't believe how she has persevered.

She changes my catheter and calls a doctor, who puts me on antibiotics. I have a lovely peaceful night. In the morning, Sarah is apologetic.

'I can't believe it took me so long,' she says. 'I'm such an idiot. I am so sorry.'

I wish I could use the spelling board to tell her how grateful I am that she took all that time to understand me, but I know if I try she will only become stressed. The truth is, many of the other nurses would simply have left. If I was in her shoes, I ask myself, would I have stayed? She didn't give up until she worked out what was wrong with me and made sure I was able to spend the night in peace. I'll make sure to tell Adrian to let her know that.

Dr Maguire arrives into my room doing his rounds.

'Good morning, Clodagh. My name is Dr Gabriel Maguire. How are you today?' He has learned to use the spelling board. He holds it up and waits for me to spell. He does his usual tests.

No, I still can't shrug my shoulders, squeeze his hand or do anything else that he asks me to do.

'The roads are closed for the Belfast Marathon,' he says in his southern lilt. 'Have you ever run in the Belfast Marathon, Clodagh?'

I spell: 'No, but I will.'

I see his face fill with pity. I don't want his pity. I spell again: 'I *will* run again. I will run part of the marathon. And I will make you do it with me.'

Reading the board, he doesn't react. But I can read what his eyes say: *No, you won't.*

You're wrong, I think to myself. *You have to be wrong. I can't imagine a future where I can't talk, can't move and can't run.*

CHAPTER NINE

I Am Locked In

A wheelchair has arrived. It sits in the corner of my room – a black monstrosity. It's huge and bulky, with padded support around it. It's the first thing I see every morning when I open my eyes. I hate it. I don't understand why it's here. Am I not going to get better? Am I not going home soon? Back to my life, to running, to work?

Everyone is behaving like getting the wheelchair is the greatest thing ever. I don't understand. The occupational therapist who arrived into my room pushing it had a look on her face that made me think she felt like Father Christmas delivering a much-wanted present.

'Soon you'll be able to use it, Clodagh,' she says. I wonder how, given that I can't so much as sit up in bed, I'm supposed to sit in this monstrosity. The sight of it makes my heart lurch and my stomach churn. I spell this out to Adrian and ask him to move it out of my sight.

But even he is behaving like it's a great thing.

'Clodagh. Don't you see? The wheelchair means freedom. I will be able to take you off the ward. We can go to the café; we can go out to the garden. When you're up to it, I can bring the kids and they can push you. We can go for walks.'

What does he mean? He is talking like a wheelchair is forever. I decide to drop the subject. Everyone else can get as excited as they like by this development but I don't know what's so thrilling about it.

The morning arrives. The occupational therapist, accompanied by her young assistant, wheel in a hoist – a weird purple metal contraption that they use to move me around in physiotherapy. It has a pale-blue parachute attached to it.

'OK, Clodagh. Are you ready?'

I can't wait, I want to reply. *It's a moment I've been waiting for all my life – sitting in the biggest, ugliest wheelchair I've ever seen!* My own sarcasm makes me smile.

I blink once.

They roll me onto my side so that the parachute can be positioned under my body. They roll me onto my back again and place my arms across my chest. A button is pressed, there is a whirr and slowly I'm lifted off the bed into the air. I feel like I'm in Barry's amusements in Portrush.

The occupational therapist tells her assistant to hold my arms because she is struggling to hold my head. I feel my arms wanting to flop. My head is so heavy. It feels like a bowling bowl on top of my shoulders. I feel like my neck will break if they let go of my head. Another button is pressed and I'm lowered down, down into the wheelchair.

For a minute it doesn't feel like the worst thing in the world. I'm sitting upright. I had worried I would fall over. But I'm a dead weight and in no time I hurt, everywhere. My head spins, I feel hot and I think I might vomit. I blink frantically at the occupational therapists. When the young assistant uses the spelling board, I spell, 'Please put me back in bed.'

'Clodagh, I know it doesn't feel great, but it's really important to get you sitting,' says the occupational therapist. 'It keeps your organs functioning properly and it helps your core.'

I blink once. I'll stay in the wheelchair. I need to think of this as gym time. If I work through the misery, I *will* get well.

Adrian smiles the first time he sees me sitting in the wheelchair.

'Brilliant, Clodagh,' he says. Then he notices my tears. 'What's wrong?'

I blink frantically and he gets the spelling board.

'My bum is agony. Get a nurse.'

Adrian hurries to get a nurse but when he returns he looks apologetic.

'They're all busy.'

I cry harder – or rather, open my mouth wider to show my distress.

'Is it that bad?' Adrian asks.

I blink frantically. I feel like my spine is about to rip through the bottom of my back. My bum cheeks feel as if they have been covered in acid. He understands my blinks and tries to lift me out of the wheelchair, but that doesn't work. I'm too heavy. He pulls my head tight into his chest and puts both his arms round my back. I feel him position his hands under both my bum cheeks. He begins to massage them. It feels wonderful. The pain begins to subside. My tears stop and I close my mouth.

A nurse walks into the room.

'Sorry,' I hear her say, and she quickly walks out again. Adrian laughs.

'Her face!' he says. 'She thinks we're up to some really weird stuff here.'

I laugh. I don't care what anyone thinks. My bum was in agony. I am in shock at the pain you can feel just because you can't adjust your position. I never imagined that sitting in a wheelchair could be so sore.

Adrian wipes my face with a cloth. It's wet with tears and saliva. My mouth is no longer dry – I can produce saliva now. In fact, I drool continuously. I try to picture myself – a still, silent creature in a ginormous wheelchair, with greasy hair pulled back into a lumpy pony tail, drooling, my own urine hanging in a bag beside me.

Maybe Adrian will leave me if I stay like this. We aren't married, after all; we haven't taken vows for better or worse. This is the first time I've really thought about this. I suppose it's been at the back of my mind, but it's the wheelchair that really throws it into relief. Adrian and I used to run together. Will he really want to push me around in a wheelchair?

But I need him to stay. Only Adrian and Diane understand me. They are the two people I need to see every day. They are my voice to the medical staff. Without them I don't know how I'll get through this.

They both have the same routine when they visit. They start at the top of my head, checking my hair, tying it high so that my bun doesn't burn into the back of my head. Then they move to my shoulders and my arms, setting them exactly where I ask on the bed. They really have the patience of saints, waiting calmly as I spell: 'Higher ... a bit to the left ... down a bit,' until I am happy. Making me comfortable is an extremely slow process.

My heels are the worst. I can't believe how much they burn. I feel like they might fall through the bed. I ask Adrian and Diane to lift my feet and rub them. They place a pillow under my calves to keep my heels off the bottom sheet. It makes all the difference. Diane announces with a smile one afternoon, 'I'm renaming the spelling board the *bossy board*!'

As I lie alone one evening after my dinner, staring at the ceiling, lost in my own thoughts, I hear a voice I recognise. It's Elizabeth, the deputy sister. I like her. When she gets time in her day she will come and massage some of the expensive lotions I seem to be acquiring into my limp hands.

'Clodagh, there's someone I'd like you to meet.' Leaning over the bed, she says, 'We've got another patient who is locked in, just like you. Would you like to meet her?'

I blink once, but in my head, I'm thinking, *What did she say? Locked in? What is locked in? Is that a type of stroke? Am I locked in? Is that what's wrong with me? Why hasn't Diane or Adrian told me? Why has nobody used those words before?*

'Locked in.' The phrase hits me like a brick to the head. I've heard it before. I remember. Tony Nicklinson. He made the news a few years ago in England. He had a stroke. He was in a wheelchair like mine. He couldn't move or talk. And he couldn't bear it. He was in the news because he was campaigning for assisted suicide. He had to, because he couldn't kill himself. But he wanted to die because he was never getting better.

That can't be me, I think. *It just can't!*

That book I read, *The Diving Bell and the Butterfly*. They made a movie of it. I thought it was sad but beautiful. The man who wrote that was locked in too! He had to write his book one blink at a time. He never walked or talked again before he died. This cannot be what is wrong with me!

I am trapped in my body. I am locked in.

My mind is racing when I hear Elizabeth's voice.

'This is Esther.' Esther and I look at each other and cry. She is older than me – I'd say 50 or 60, at a guess. Her eyes look alive and she scrutinises me keenly, but she is slumped like a sack of potatoes. Her body is inert.

I look at her, at her lined face, at her hair, greying at the roots, and I think, *But the same thing can't be wrong with me. I can't be like her, like Tony Nicklinson. I'm much younger than them. That kind of thing just doesn't happen to people like me – I'm an ordinary woman and I'm fit!*

But I *am* just like Esther. I'm slumped and inert too. I'm never getting better!

By the time Diane arrives I am inconsolable. Diane hates my silent crying. She tells me it is the most awful thing she has ever had to watch. I don't care. I hate her. It's her fault I'm going to have to live like this forever. I was happy to die in A & E. I still want to die. And I can't even kill myself!

'Please, Clodagh, stop this. Tell me what is wrong.' Diane's voice is close to breaking. She wipes away my tears. She holds the spelling board.

I stare at the board angrily and begin spelling.

'This is your fault. I'm going to be like this forever. You should not have saved me.'

Diane sits on the edge of my bed and holds my hand. She looks into my eyes.

'I know you are going to be okay. If you weren't, God wouldn't have let me save you. I shouted and you came back. I didn't do that for you to give up on me now. You *will* fight this. I know you will. You've got that tracheostomy thing out. You can swallow. You have to be patient. It will be slow – but I know you will get better!'

Diane stops talking. My room is filled with silence. There is activity in the corridors, with evening visitors. I stare at the ceiling. The irony of the whole situation. When I was on duty I'd be called to bridges in the city to persuade suicidal people not to jump. I stopped them from killing themselves. Now I'm the one that needs talking down. Yet I couldn't even throw myself off this bed if I wanted to.

Diane interrupts my thoughts.

'I read on the internet about a young girl called Leah. She had the same thing as you a few years ago. She's amazing. She can talk, she can drive, she even went to South Africa. It all started with a finger moving.'

I wanted to ask Diane whether the girl was now running four miles a day. And if not, why was she telling me this? If it was to make me feel better, she was wasting her breath.

Diane is like Adrian – she can read my mind.

'No, Clodagh, she doesn't run four miles a day. Why would anyone want to run four miles a day?' She continues gently to tell me Leah's story, sounding impressed by this girl as she talks.

And, in that moment, Leah's story transforms the complete hopelessness I've been feeling into optimism. I will recover. I wanted to give up, I wanted to die. All these people helping me to beat this and I can't even say thank you. But I will. I will talk again. I will say thank you to each of them.

My occupational therapist would like me to try sitting in a normal chair. I'm not convinced I'll be able to. But, when she arrives with a mustard-coloured wing-backed chair almost as ugly as my wheelchair, I realise she doesn't mean 'normal'. What she means is something other than a wheelchair.

Mum and Dad arrive as I lie splayed in the chair. The occupational therapist has attempted to make me look like I'm sitting by propping me up with pillows at each side. But the sight of me upsets my mum. Poor Mum. Every day she brings in new pyjamas for me or expensive creams. She spends so much money. She'd give me the world if she could. She'd do anything in her power to make me better, but she's scared of me. Scared to touch me, scared to communicate with me.

This is heartbreaking for me. I want to tell her I will be okay, to stop worrying about me, to talk to me like she always has.

I'm still Clodagh, your feisty daughter! I want to tell her. But I know she loves me dearly.

When Adrian arrives, he and Dad go outside for a smoke, leaving Mum sitting there, staring at me. She looks lost. Adrian hands her the board and says, 'You can have a nice chat with Clodagh.'

She holds up the board and says, 'How are you today?' Her voice is so loud – and her enunciation so slow and clear. Does she think I'm deaf along with everything else? She doesn't look at me, but peers around the room. Then there's silence.

We remain in silence until Adrian and Dad return. Adrian and I talk on the board – and I spell, 'Tell her I'm not bloody deaf. It's just me. Talk normally.'

He turns to Mum and, disregarding what I've written, says, 'Clodagh says you have to learn to use the board. She's promised to be patient.' He glares at me. I know that look. It means he's serious.

Adrian hands Mum the spelling board. We start practising.

'Something simple, like hello,' he says with a Sergeant Simpson tone in his voice. I spell out, 'Hello,' and we progress to, 'I am Clodagh.' At first she makes mistakes, but gradually she becomes more comfortable with it; and when she gets things wrong, she laughs at herself.

When visiting ends, as my mum and dad leave, I can see that their faces look happier. This is the first time we have all laughed. This is the first time they have treated me as Clodagh. My heart surges with love for them. And for Adrian and Diane. They really have so much patience with me.

Now Mum can use the spelling board, her visits are no longer painful. Mum tells me she hates using the board but I tell her not to worry if she gets something wrong. I spell out: 'Can you ask Dad to read the paper to me?'

It becomes a daily ritual. My dad sits on the bed and reads stories from the daily newspaper to me. I can see it makes him as happy as it makes me. It makes him feel less helpless.

Not that using the spelling board always goes smoothly. As Adrian leaves my room to go for a smoke, he warns me to be patient with my parents. I try to follow his instructions, but it's frustrating when I can't get my point across.

I can't make strong facial expressions yet. My smile isn't big, and I can't frown, so when I'm trying to be funny I use 'LOL'. Anger is harder. I have to use swear words to show it. When I spell out the word 'fuck', Mum is furious.

'Clodagh Dunlop! Don't use words like that!' she shouts.

Dad lifts his head from the newspaper he is reading.

'Your mother's right. You were never taught to use language like that. It's vulgar.'

It's a relief when Diane enters the room, carrying Hannah, her youngest daughter. Hannah is three.

'Say hello to Auntie Clodagh,' she says. But Hannah stares at me, looking terrified. She clings to Diane's legs. Since my stroke, my nephew and nieces have been kept away from the hospital. Diane has made videos with them every day and showed them to me on her mobile phone during visiting. In the videos they laugh and shout, 'Get well soon! We love you, Auntie Clodagh!'

I stare at Hannah. I can't say hello. I can't pick her up and give her a hug. Hannah begins to scream in terror. She doesn't know me. I cry, and she cries harder. Neither of us can stop. It's heartbreaking. My own niece is frightened of the sight of me.

'Clodagh, stop, please. I'm so sorry!' sobs Diane. Mum scoops up Hannah, who is still screaming. They leave my room. Slowly, the screams disappear.

I am inconsolable. Diane puts her arms around me. She sobs, apologising time and time again.

'I didn't think. I thought I was doing a good thing!' She can barely talk through her sobs. 'I won't bring her again. Or Emily or Adam.'

When we eventually stop crying, Diane holds up the spelling board.

'Look at me! I'm a monster. I want to die!' I spell.

'Stop that nonsense. So you have bad hair right now, but you can sit up! You will talk again. You will walk. Damn it, girl, you'll run again! I promise. And you know it, too!'

Diane and I begin to laugh. I spell out, 'If I don't, you have to look after me. This whole mess is your fault.'

Wiping my face like I'm one of her kids, she says, 'You know I will.'

A few days later I see why Hannah was so scared. I finish my physiotherapy and Adrian is with me, as he is every day in physiotherapy. The physio assistant asks if I would like to see outside the stroke ward. I blink once. I don't particularly want to – I know that if I'm in the large black wheelchair people will stare. I don't want to be stared at. But I know Adrian wants me to say yes.

She pushes my wheelchair out into the long glass corridors of the Royal Victoria Hospital. There are windows all around and Adrian suggests that he open one so I can feel the air outside. As I'm positioned at the window I'm transfixed by the sight of a slumped creature with a lolling head, drooling mouth hanging open, hair all askew. I shudder.

I keep looking. The lolling creature is me. I look even worse than I imagined. It can't be me! I don't recognise myself. I'm scared. Terrified – of myself. I'm locked in!

I'm not going to Fiona's wedding. I'm not going anywhere ever again.

CHAPTER TEN

Breaking Out

I love birthdays. Especially *my* birthday. My mum always makes a fuss and makes me feel special. The last birthday before my stroke – my thirty-fifth – was no different. It started with my favourite breakfast – poached eggs and toast – cooked by Adrian. Later in the day, Mum arrived with her arms full of presents and the obligatory birthday cake.

After, Adrian and I went to our favourite restaurant. When we got home we opened a bottle of wine and danced in the kitchen to our 'dance me' music. It really was a perfect day.

My thirty-sixth birthday, however, is going to be completely different.

My birthday is on a Friday. I would like Adrian to spend the day with me in hospital, but that isn't possible. His dad is celebrating his seventieth birthday in a local hotel. It was organised months ago. I'm supposed to be there with Adrian. He said he'd stay with me at the hospital if that's what I want, but I don't want him to miss his dad's special birthday.

I wake and immediately feel sad. The nurses burst into my room, singing 'Happy Birthday' at the top of their voices. They blow up balloons and hang banners around. They bring me a present. I appreciate it – all this trouble to make the day special for me – but it makes me think of all the things I can't do. I can't blow out candles on a cake. I definitely can't eat cake – I would choke and it would probably kill me. And I can't open my own presents because my body still doesn't move.

I've never had so many presents. They pour in from my family, friends and colleagues; from relatives who have never given me a birthday gift before; from the families of other patients; and from the nurses. I get pyjamas, jewellery, expensive creams and much more. I would have loved all these gifts before I became locked in. Now it's just stuff.

Adrian comes in after lunch to wish me happy birthday before his dad's party. He brings a stack of birthday cards – some from work, others that have arrived in the post from people I barely know. He opens them and sets them on every available surface. A nurse pops her head in and, laughing, says, 'My word, Clodagh! Look at the number of cards!'

Later, Diane and her husband, David, visit. And before they leave, KD arrives. She's told Adrian that she's read a book all about locked-in syndrome so that she can be the ideal best friend. She has a romantic vision of it – and of how she will make my life better.

I love her. She's fabulous. We clicked the moment we met at university and, since then, we've shared lots of adventures. I was bridesmaid at her wedding last year. She's scarily clever. In spite of that, I'm the strong one in our friendship. She might have brains to burn but, when it comes to common sense, I can run circles round her.

When Diane and David leave, KD picks up the spelling board. She's getting better at using it but I know it makes her nervous. Adrian has warned me to be patient with her. I'm glad she's here with me. Since my tracheostomy tube was removed, I have been strengthening my swallow. But I have a lot of tablets to take – blood thinners, muscle relaxants, stomach medication and painkillers – and I still need thickened fluids when I take them. One nurse in particular doesn't seem to realise this, despite it being written in capital letters above my bed. I'm terrified of choking to death. I have heard her voice tonight in the corridors and it frightens me.

I begin to spell out, 'Will you give me my tablets?' but KD doesn't let me finish the sentence. She's too impulsive; she thinks she knows what I'm going to spell. She says, 'What do you want off the table?'

I spell: 'Let me finish. Don't predict what I'm spelling.'

'Okay, pet, I'm sorry. I'm useless at this.' She's becoming flushed with anxiety; her glasses have slipped down her nose and she has taken off her cardigan. She's determined to get this right. She stands poised, looking at me, with the spelling board. 'Okay, pet, let's try again.'

I spell: 'Will you get me my table—'

KD stares at the board, puzzled.

'What do you want from the table?' She hasn't waited for me to finish spelling 'tablets'.

KD begins picking up items from the locker beside my bed.

'Do you want this, pet? Or this?' she picks up every item on the locker and, every time she asks is it the right item, I blink twice. We are both becoming more distressed.

'I'll get this. Try again,' she says. Her voice has become wobbly and high pitched.

I spell: 'Let me finish spelling. Stop predicting.'

I can tell KD is on the verge of breaking down, but I don't care. Blinking each letter of every word that I want to say is frustrating at the best of times. It's even worse when the other person doesn't understand what I have painstakingly spelt out. I'm furious with KD. How can someone so intelligent be so stupid?

'Right. We'll get this, I promise, pet.' Her face is red and her eyes are filled with tears. I want to scream at her and tell her she's an idiot. It's 11 o'clock at night; the nurse will be here soon with my tablets. I don't want to choke to death on my birthday.

I start to spell again: 'Will you get me my table—'

KD bursts into tears.

'I don't know what you want from the table!'

I want to get out of my bed and shake her. I am so angry with her. I scream at her with everything I have: 'Ahhhhhhhhhhhh!' I raise my arms. I am going to strangle her. I keep screaming at her. KD stands, sobbing, beside my bed, the spelling board still in her hands.

Nurses begin to appear from every direction. They run in, breathless with panic.

'What on earth is wrong? What's this noise about?' asks one of the nurses.

'Clodagh, calm down. We'll get whatever it is,' says another, wiping my eyes. She takes the spelling board from KD. 'Okay. Take your time.'

I spell out: 'Tablets.'

KD is drying her eyes.

'Tablets. Not table. I'm sorry.'

Calm begins to return to my room. The nurse says, 'Let me get this right. Who was it making that horrendous noise?'

'Clodagh!' says KD, putting her hand to her mouth in shock. I look at her, she looks at me, and realisation dawns. She begins to laugh. I laugh too. I am producing sound! I can hear the strange noise coming from me and it makes me laugh more.

'*And* her arms moved,' says KD, who, sounding shell-shocked, is still laughing.

We all look at each other. The nurses laugh too. Everyone realises what a significant moment this is. When we all calm down, the nurses leave my room. The news spreads around the ward like wildfire.

'Adrian needs to know about this,' says KD. 'I'll take a video of you – then he can see it for himself.' She aims her phone at me. I make my arms move, albeit maybe less than half a centimetre, and make some noise.

KD raises her eyebrows.

'Clodagh, you sound like a dying pig. But it's the best noise I have ever heard.'

She tries to ring Adrian to give him the news, but his phone goes to voicemail, so she sends him the video with a short explanation. KD is about to leave when he rings back. She talks to him, telling him the whole story, then shuts off her phone.

'He got the message when he went upstairs for a smoke,' she tells me. 'He's so happy – you have no idea! He can't wait to come in and hear for himself.'

When KD has left, I stare at the ceiling and try to use my voice again. I'm terrified it will stop, but the sound comes out.

'Ahhhhhh!' I'm so happy. I try to move my arms and they move just a little. I can't believe it. This is the best birthday present *ever*!

The news spreads around the stroke ward. On Monday morning Sarah-Jane walks into my room. I have been excited all weekend for her to hear my sound.

'Say ah, Clodagh.'

'Ahhhhhh.'

'Now try ooh.' She rounds her lips.

'Ahhhhhh.' I can't round my lips.

'Try eeh,' says Sarah-Jane, widening her mouth as much as she can.

'Ahhhhhh.'

It's one thing being able to make noise; it's quite another being able to talk. I begin to cry. I sound like a wolf howling.

Concerned, she holds up the spelling board.

'Why are you crying, Clodagh?'

'I have no idea,' I spell out. And that's the truth. I know that I'm not going to be able to talk as quickly as I'd hoped, that learning to talk again will take hard work, but that's not really enough to set me howling like I am now. I spell: 'I don't understand why I cry so much.'

Putting down the spelling board, Sarah-Jane sits on the mustard-coloured chair.

'Has anyone explained the concept of emotional lability to you, Clodagh?' I blink twice.

'It can happen after a stroke,' she says. 'It's as if your emotional filters have broken. Your emotions are exaggerated – you can find yourself crying or laughing uncontrollably a lot of the time. Sometimes the emotions displayed are greater than the emotions you are feeling. It's normal, Clodagh. It dampens with time. Don't worry about it. Okay?'

Hearing this explanation, I want to jump out of bed and give Sarah-Jane a big hug. It makes so much sense. I don't normally cry or laugh as much as I have since the stroke. These huge displays of emotion don't reflect my feelings. I hate this. I like to be in control of everything and not to be in control of my emotions is horrible.

Still, I'm relieved that I now understand why. And, when Adrian comes in, it's the first thing I spell out to him. But I can't get him to understand.

'I know why you're crying, Clodagh,' he says. 'You're upset because you have to lie here like this.'

I'm about to lose my patience when Sarah-Jane comes back into the room. I blink frantically, then spell to her, asking her to explain emotional lability to Adrian. She does.

'Okay,' he says. 'I understand that. But does she have to accept that? I mean, is there anything she can do to help control it? Or anything I can do?'

'Well, some people manage to tone it down with practice. It's a question of turning your mind to something else. And, anyway, it should ease off with time.'

It's a huge relief to both of us to hear this.

Now that I can make noise and have a little movement in my arms, I feel more optimistic. Maybe Adrian and Diane are right – I will be okay. I have to work at getting better, that's all. There is no magic cure.

Until now I just couldn't have coped with visitors from outside the family. It's hard dealing with people's distress when you're struggling to come to terms with your condition. But now I decide it's time.

I start with my stepdaughter, Caoimhe. I love Caoimhe. She is smart and beautiful. I'm always surprised by how wise she is, despite her being a teenager. We've always enjoyed the time we've spent together. She arrives with Adrian one afternoon, wearing her blue school uniform, her long black hair glossy. I worry. Will she cope? How will she react to the creature I've become? Will the shock make her freak out in another version of that horrendous scene with Hannah?

She doesn't cry. That's a good start. She just smiles and starts chatting, her words falling over each other. She talks about the times when I would run and she would cycle beside me.

'We'll be doing that again, Clodagh,' she says. 'We will. I *know* we will.'

Adrian chats to me. He asks whether occupational therapy have made the hand splint they were talking about. We discuss the new exercises Sarah-Jane has shown me. He begins to talk about his plans with Caoimhe at the weekend. But I see her standing at the end of my bed. She has gone deathly white. She begins to sway. I blink frantically at Adrian, trying to warn him. He holds up the spelling board.

'What is it, Clodagh?'

There isn't time to spell it out. I'm frantic. I keep blinking, hoping he understands that something is wrong. He does. He turns, shouts out in alarm and catches Caoimhe just before she hits the ground. A nurse appears, having heard the commotion, and takes over. Sitting Caoimhe down, she puts her head between her knees, while Adrian pours a glass of water.

I can only lie and watch. I hate that I'm so helpless. I'm supposed to look after Caoimhe, and now there's nothing I can do.

When Caoimhe's colour returns, and the nurse leaves, Adrian holds up the spelling board and I spell: 'Caoimhe just wants attention. She is trying to steal my thunder.' Caoimhe laughs. I need her to see that, in spite of everything, I am still the same Clodagh. I can still joke around and tease her. I am still me.

When Adrian next visits he tells me that Fiona and Damien want to come and see me. Fiona has kept in close contact with Adrian throughout.

'They're just back from their honeymoon,' he says, 'and they want to show you the pictures. Can they visit?'

I blink: *yes*. I don't think twice. It will be hard letting Fiona see me like this, but I've missed her. I've missed everyone at work.

The night of their visit, Adrian arrives first. He looks at me with a serious face. 'Are you still okay for Fi and Damien to come tonight?'

I blink once. I'm excited to see them.

'Dinger is with them. He's asked can he come in. Is that okay?'

Dinger is another colleague from my section. I blink once.

Adrian leaves my room and returns with all three of them. Fiona comes in, smiling, kissing me, treating me exactly the same as she always has. She's carrying some flowers.

'These were a centrepiece at the wedding,' she says. 'Shall I put them on your locker, darling Clodagh?' She holds my hand. 'I'm so sorry you couldn't be there. I've missed you so much. We all have.' She turns to look at Damien and Dinger.

'You've pulled some stunt to get out of a 70 obs turn, mate!' says Dinger, looking at me with a cheeky grin on his face. Every police officer dreads being detailed 70 observer for a shift. The 70 observer will be the first responder to everything. It is renowned among police officers as the worst duty turn.

'Dinger!' exclaims Fiona. Adrian and Damien laugh. I haven't heard Adrian laugh so heartily since I had the stroke.

Undeterred, Dinger says, 'I'm serious, mate. It's a bit over the top.'

I'm so glad I've let them visit. They've taken the Clodagh lying slouched in front of them in their stride. Whatever they are thinking, they are concealing it brilliantly. Their chatter fills my room. Fiona perches on my bed and says, 'Damien, give me the wedding album to show Clodagh. You boys are useless.'

The album is lovely. Fiona turns the pages, showing me photographs from the day. She looks stunning. I knew she would. I cry. I hope she knows it's because I'm happy for her.

'I've got some bad news, though,' she says when we are finished. 'Mr Blond has died.' Mr Blond is her cat. She loved him and owned him for 14 years. Everyone in our work section knew Mr Blond.

I begin to laugh. The men begin to laugh too.

'It's terrible! Oh, you are all so terrible,' protests Fiona, but she is smiling too. As we laugh at her silliness, I think how much my room has needed the energy they have brought with their visit. When they leave, and I'm settled for the night, I lie and plan more visitors. I miss the people from my life.

The next day, Adrian and KD arrive. Adrian has had the same thoughts as me after last night's visitors. He says, 'We've brought Kris, too. He's waiting outside in the corridor. Can he come in?'

I blink once. I like KD's husband, Kris. Unlike last night's visitors, I see shock in his eyes when he comes in. He's nervous. Slumped in my wheelchair, I'm not the Clodagh he remembers.

Adrian hands him the spelling board and shows him how it works. I need to make him see I'm still Clodagh. My body doesn't work now, that's all. I need an icebreaker. I smile to myself: I know the very one. I spell out: 'Hi, Kris. I have shat myself.'

He reads it out, but turns red.

'I think I've got that wrong,' he says. Kris holds the spelling board up to try again, his face full of concentration.

I spell: 'Kris, I have shat myself.'

He puts down the board and begins to laugh.

'Aw, Clodes, you're winding me up!'

The others are in fits of laughter.

'Kris, who knew you were such a great laxative?' says KD when she stops laughing.

Adrian whispers in my ear, 'You are bad!' He leaves, laughing, to find a nurse to change me. I don't usually broadcast my bowel movements, but I knew humour would make Kris relax.

The afternoon is spent in conversation and laughter with friends. I miss the world outside the stroke ward.

I now understand that I have locked-in syndrome. I don't have flu – I'm not going to recover in a few days. It's going to take a long time. I've overheard conversations in the corridor that make it sound like my life is over. It's terrible, the voices say, that this has happened to someone so young. She used to be a police officer, they say.

Whenever I ask questions about when I will talk and walk again, the medical staff, my family and even Adrian avoid answering me. Everyone seems to accept that the wheelchair is permanent. I know what they are all thinking. But I know I will recover. I will show them all! I will talk, I will walk and I will return to duty.

The visits from my friends over the past few days have made me realise how much I miss the people I know. I have used Facebook to keep in contact with family who live abroad and people I've met travelling. I feel so isolated from my previous life, it occurs to me that I can use it to reach out to people. I'll start a Facebook page.

I think it's a brilliant idea. For a start, it would be a way for me to stay in contact with people. Adrian tells me every day that everyone is asking how I am. Diane and Mum tell me the same. I want to tell people myself. I know it upsets my mum when people ask her about me. By sharing my recovery on Facebook, people won't need to ask her questions.

A Facebook page would protect me, too. When I'm home and in a wheelchair, people will stare. They'll wonder what is wrong with me. But if I share what is wrong with me, they won't *need* to ask me what has happened. They won't stare.

And, by sharing what has happened to me, I might also be able to raise awareness of the fact that young people can have strokes. I was ignorant before it happened to me. People *should* know.

I talk about it with Adrian when he next visits.

'I want a Facebook page,' I spell.

I expect him to agree that it's a good idea, but he looks doubtful.

'Your family won't want that.'

'What's it got to do with them?' I spell. I am annoyed with Adrian, I am my own person; I know my own mind.

'You know your parents are trying to come to terms with your illness. It's hard for them to get their head around it.'

I do know that – and it annoys me. It's me who has suffered a stroke. It's me who might be locked in forever. I am trying to get my head around this illness too. Do I embarrass them?

'Adrian, it is my illness. My Facebook page. I want to tell my friends about my recovery. Please, will you set it up?' I'm getting more and more annoyed with Adrian. Carefully blinking out every letter to win the argument feels pointless when Adrian lowers the spelling board. I can't stop him from having the last word.

'I will have to talk to Diane first.'

That makes me see red. *I'm* the older sister – the one who makes decisions, the one who looks after her. She is the baby of the family. I hate that our roles have been reversed. Reluctantly I agree. I know I will get my way in the end. But the problem is that Adrian and Diane's visits never coincide. We fight about it for a week. If he won't set up the page, I tell Adrian, I'll get Diane to do it. But he's still not sure it's the right thing to do. He goes on talking about my parents and how they won't want it.

I feel helpless. I don't care what Mum and Dad think. This is important to me. I have locked-in syndrome. It's bad enough that my own body is holding me prisoner. Now I'm being held prisoner by my own family, who won't let me talk to my friends!

Finally, Adrian and Diane visit at the same time. I spell out to them both on the spelling board: 'I want a Facebook page.'

'I'm sorry, Diane,' says Adrian with a sigh. 'I've told her I won't do it without your family's permission – and I know I won't get it.'

I want to scream at Adrian: *I am asking you! I am an adult. You don't need their permission.*

'Ahhhhhhhhhhhh!'

Both of them look at me and speak to me in raised voices at the same time.

'Okay, Clodagh, okay! You can have a Facebook page,' says Diane.

'Right, Clodagh, okay! Now stop that screaming!' says Adrian. He looks annoyed, but I don't care. They have agreed I can have a Facebook page. I have won!

I want to get it started as soon as possible. On 11 May, my last night in the Royal, we put up our first post. Adrian props me up on the bed and places a sign in front of me, with #beatinglockedin written on it. In the photograph I'm wearing pyjamas, there's a red mark on my neck from the tracheostomy and my fingers are swollen. It's not a great picture but it will do.

I'm surprised by the reaction. The picture gets over 200 likes. This confirms that sharing my recovery was the right decision.

'It's amazing,' says Adrian, when he shows me the reaction. 'But it's a leap of faith. You now have to show your followers how far you can progress.'

He's right. But that's the point of it. It might take time, but there isn't any part of me that's in doubt any more. I *will* recover.

CHAPTER ELEVEN

Moving On

It's six weeks since I had a stroke and I'm leaving the Royal Victoria Hospital. Now that the tracheostomy tube has been removed and I can swallow puréed food, I'm considered well enough to move on to rehabilitation, and I'm off to Belfast's Regional Acquired Brain Injury Unit, or RABIU for short. I'm excited to get there. Everyone has told me they work miracles.

'RABIU really is brilliant,' Kerry says. 'I did a placement there as a student nurse. They can do extraordinary things!'

The nurses and therapists come out to the corridors and wave goodbye as I leave.

'Good luck, Clodagh!' they say. Some promise to visit me, and say, 'We'll miss you!'

I'd like to spell out 'Thank you,' and maybe 'Sorry for when I was a pain,' but I can't. Adrian has my spelling board and he's already left for RABIU. I offer them a smile. I'm quite sure they don't expect me to wave. Especially not when I'm wrapped tight in a white blanket with my arms pinned by my side like an Egyptian mummy.

Two paramedics come to collect me. They tighten orange straps across my body, securing me to a trolley. It's as though I'm a dangerous criminal and likely to escape. All that's missing are the handcuffs. They place themselves at each end of the trolley and talk over me as if I'm not here. They don't notice the sweat pouring down my face, into my eyes, and pooling round my neck. I stare at the paramedic at my feet, willing him to look at my eyes. But, as they wheel me down corridors, through doors and around corners, he doesn't look at me. Not once.

They push the trolley through double doors and we leave the building. There's a rush of cool air. I feel the wind on my face, and I want to shout, *Stop! Stay here for a minute. Please! I haven't been outside in six weeks.* Do they not understand that this is a momentous occasion? I just want a moment in the fresh air. I cry silently as they move across the parking area at breakneck speed and slide the stretcher into the ambulance. They don't notice my tears – or maybe they choose not to notice. A paramedic takes the driver's seat, leaving the other to sit beside me.

We take the motorway. I fill with jealousy as I look out of the ambulance window. My life has come to a crashing halt, but all these people in their cars are going about their everyday lives. They can go home, watch television, eat dinner, do whatever they want to do. When will *I* be able to go home?

The paramedic beside me stares out of the window. Why doesn't he talk to me? Staring at his face, I realise I mean nothing to him. I'm just another job. Inside I shout at him: *I'm a person. Talk to me! Tell me something! Anything! What's happening in the world? What's happening in local news? Just talk about the weather!*

I will him to say something. Although I've never met the paramedic before, it feels like we have had an argument. There's tension in the air. I'm sure he doesn't know what to say. It makes me sad to think that my very presence, my mute motionless body, is making him uncomfortable. What have I become?

The ambulance turns off the road and comes to a stop. The paramedics jump out. I'm wheeled into a curved, cream, brick building with large glass windows. The paramedics talk over me about their next job as they wheel me into an empty ward. I don't like it. I miss the stroke ward. I miss the nurses I have got to know. They won't be able to use the spelling board here – I know it.

The paramedics transfer me to a bed. Once they've finished they turn and leave without a backward glance.

The ward is large and there are only four beds. Adrian arrives minutes after me and he seems impressed. He points out the huge windows and the view of the gardens beyond. He expects me to love it all. But I don't. I hate it. I just want to go home. I've had enough of hospitals.

A medical team arrives and assembles at the end of my bed. They ask Adrian to leave.

'We're going to talk to Clodagh so that we can work out a plan of care.'

Adrian smirks. I want to shout at him, *Don't dare leave! These idiots won't know how to use my spelling board!*

Adrian holds out the spelling board. He says, 'You'll need this. It's how Clodagh communicates. Would you like me to show you how it works?'

'That won't be necessary,' the consultant says dismissively. 'We'll be able to talk to Clodagh.'

Adrian is amused. He places the board on my bedside locker and leaves. He knows, with my emotional lability, that it won't be long before I'm crying at the medical team. I stare into the faces staring back at me. There's a deputy sister, the consultant, a younger doctor and a nurse.

The young nurse doesn't talk, but quickly and efficiently puts a hospital band on my wrist, then another around my ankle. I feel like a cow being tagged before going to market.

The questions begin, but I can't answer: 'How are you getting on? What stage are you at in physiotherapy?'

Why can't you ask me closed questions that I can answer with blinks? I feel the emotions begin to bubble inside me. I begin to cry. Sometimes, now, my crying is accompanied by noise. This time there's noise. I sound like an enraged animal.

They look at each other in alarm, and the doctor says, 'I think we'd better get her partner back in here.'

A nurse hurries out to fetch Adrian. He comes in, smirking, 'I told you so' written all over his face. I stop the noise. Everyone relaxes. Adrian becomes the translator, using the spelling board to communicate between us all. When the team have all the information they need, they leave.

Adrian sits on my bed.

'You need to give this place a chance, Clodagh.'

An older nurse approaches us. She has short dark hair and her tunic is a darker shade of blue than the other nurses' tunics. There is an air about her that says, 'I'm in charge.' She introduces herself to us as the sister.

I glare at Adrian. He understands what I mean. He begins to tell her how important it is that everyone should try to learn to use the spelling board.

'Without it, Clodagh feels vulnerable. She has no way to communicate.'

The sister explains that in RABIU the staff usually communicate with patients through broken speech and writing. My condition of not making noise or being able to write is rare – quite new to the unit, in fact. But she reassures Adrian that her staff will use the spelling board and Adrian gives her a short lesson. As the sister stands practising the board with Adrian, I decide I like her. I'm quite sure she runs a tight ship here, which can only be a good thing for me.

Adrian is allowed to remain with me for the first day to help me settle in. As he spoon-feeds me another tasteless puréed dinner, I look around, taking in all I see. There is a woman in the bed next to mine. I haven't noticed her until now but she must have been here when I arrived. She's not moving. Is she locked in, like me, or just asleep?

There is nobody in the bed opposite, but the sheet is rumpled. There's a newspaper folded up on the chair and a water jug on the locker. Soon the occupant of the bed is wheeled in by a nurse. I stare over at her. She's about my age. Her head has been shaved. She has a dent in her head; part of her skull is missing. I notice that she is pregnant.

I wish I could talk. I want to ask what has happened to her. I want to ask her name, where she's from, what this place is like. She switches on her TV and I feel sorry for myself. Even if I had a TV I wouldn't be able to turn it on, never mind change the channel.

When the time comes for Adrian to leave, he kisses me on the forehead and stares into my face.

'You will be okay, pet. They promised to use the board. You are going to beat this. I will bring you home when it's time, I promise.'

I watch Adrian leave. I feel so alone. I want to go home so badly it makes my heart ache.

There is a bustle in the ward as the nurses get everyone ready for the night. One approaches me and gives me my night-time medication. Patiently, she checks I'm happy with the position of the pillows, that the sheet covering me is okay, that every part of me is comfortable.

When my head began to move a little, occupational therapy gave me a large red button. The red button was positioned next to my head. If I need or want anything I turn my head to the side and press the button. A voice recording plays, 'Hello, it's Clodagh here. Can you help me?'

The nurse checks I'm happy with the position of the red button. When I indicate that I am, she says to me, 'Do you see that window on the other side? That's the nurses' station. If you need anything in the night, press your button and I'll come to you.'

I had felt terrified that my first night in RABIU would be like my first night in the stroke ward – that no one would check that I was comfortable, that I would be alone all night. But with my red button positioned correctly and everything perfect, I feel my eyes getting heavy and sleep coming.

'I'm Alison, by the way.'

Through half-closed eyes I watch the back of Alison's blue tunic disappear from the dark ward into the brightly lit corridor. It looks like she has wings on her back. My eyes must be playing tricks on me. I feel safe with Alison.

I soon learn the routine in RABIU. There are three types of therapy throughout the day – occupational therapy, physiotherapy and speech-and-language therapy. There are scheduled rest times and scheduled times when we sit in our wheelchairs. We must wear clothes; we don't wear pyjamas throughout the day. Meals are not to be eaten in bed. Everyone must attend the dining room for breakfast, lunch and dinner.

Speech and language visit the dining room at mealtimes. An imposing whiteboard hangs on a wall in the dining room. On it is listed every patient's name and, beside each name, what diet has been approved by speech and language. I am still on a puréed diet. A nurse spoon-feeds me my meals. I envy those patients with a normal diet and the ones who can feed themselves, but I'm grateful that I don't have to get liquid through a peg in my stomach like some others.

Speech-and-language therapy soon becomes my favourite part of the day. I am determined to talk again and Bronagh, my speech therapist, is always fun. She is a country girl who talks about her 'mammy'. She looks remarkably like Hollywood actress Isla Fisher, with her long copper hair.

Bronagh takes me to the garden, where we sit under a large tree, and teaches me different sounds. I'm trying to make 'b' and 'k' sounds. I try so hard, but I can't manage it. My tongue still won't work, although I'm get better at making noise. I practise all day, every day. I shout, 'Ahhhhhh!' as loud as I can. The nurses come running.

'What's wrong, Clodagh?'

When I let her know there's nothing wrong, a nurse tells me, 'You sound out of control, shouting like that.' I don't care. I mustn't care. If I concentrate on making sounds – if I practise and practise – I'll be able to talk properly. I miss talking so much!

Lesley in my ward has had a stroke too and, although she can talk, she needs to strengthen her vocal cords. She makes me laugh. Listening to me shouting, 'Ahhhhhh!' hour after hour, she starts to join in.

'You are Chewbacca!' she yells. 'Chewbacca! Chewbacca!'

Diane walks into the ward. She laughs.

'You two sound wild, shouting like that!' She pauses. 'Though, now that you mention it, Lesley, Clodagh does sound like Chewbacca from *Star Wars*! Poor Lisa!'

Diane has a routine when she visits me in RABIU. She calls herself my beautician. She begins to spray dry shampoo on me and brushes my hair.

'Lisa breaks my heart,' she says. 'Here she is, alone, at this special time in her life. She can't be at home with her husband. Can you imagine it? She has a one-year-old son! And she has to listen to you – a screaming banshee!'

Diane moves towards my face with tweezers in her hand. I feel a sharp nip as she plucks a stray hair from my eyebrow. It makes me yelp.

'Do you think if I plucked every hair from your eyebrows you'd start talking?' Diane laughs.

I live for Diane's visits, but I have developed a phobia about them. I worry she will be killed on the motorway. She's not the greatest driver in the world. She's almost always late. If she's due to visit at six o'clock, she won't make it until a quarter past. I watch the clock and, as soon as six o'clock comes and goes, I start shouting. I make noise as I try to say, 'Diane is dead. She's dead!' She says my roars meet her as she runs in the doors of RABIU.

'I'm sorry, Clodagh! It was the traffic.'

The terror that she might die is genuine. I don't think she gets it – not really.

Now I've learnt the name of the pregnant woman with the shaved hair and the dent in her head. It's Lisa. As if sensing that I want to know how she's ended up here, Lisa tells me in the dining room.

'The doctors didn't realise what was wrong. I bled out into my brain and had to have parts of it removed. But they're going to sort out this dent in my head – once the baby arrives.' She places her one functioning hand protectively on her small bump.

Lisa talks to me every day when we're not at therapy. She tries to work out what I'm saying. She has endless patience. I really like her. She's engaging with me, like any friend would. Life is starting to feel better.

I still have moments of despair, of wondering if I'll ever manage language again, but then I look at Mary in the bed next to me. Mary has had a severe stroke too. She's been in hospital for 13 months – more than a year. She isn't locked in, but she still has no speech or movement. I can't imagine that. Mary is older than me, but still young at 49, with much of her life ahead of her. She can't communicate in any way. I ask the speech therapists why they haven't tried a spelling board.

'Mary's stroke is different from yours,' they say. 'Her stroke has affected a different part of her brain. But we will find a way to communicate with her.'

Being in rehabilitation is very different to the relaxed routine I had in the stroke ward. There's a timetable to make sure that it runs smoothly and, to make sure therapy isn't interrupted with lengthy toilet breaks, they give the patients an enema every night.

I hate enema time. A cardboard bedpan hurts when your body is a dead weight and you can't shift your bum. One night the nurses leave me on the bedpan for 45 minutes. It's unbearable. I try to moan and scream, desperate for someone to notice. But my voice tires at night and, anyway, the nurses have been called to another patient. I can hear them all running. An alarm is sounding. Realising there's some kind of emergency, I feel sad – and not just for the patient. It is a reminder of my work as a police officer. Just a few months ago I was the one running to save lives.

I think about one particular incident. It was the late shift on a Saturday, and

I'd been dispatched, along with a colleague, to a 'concern for safety' call on the edge of a republican estate. A man was threatening to hang himself. Sometimes these calls were cries for help – people just needed someone to talk to – but it was always possible that they'd carry out their threat. So, in order to preserve life, you had to respond at once.

I knew how serious this kind of job was, but the child in me loved it. As the driver, it meant turning on the sirens and the blue lights as I sped through the city in an armoured police car. I never tired of the experience. Each call was as exciting as the first one. My heart beat a little faster, but I had to concentrate, reading the road, trying to predict what way other drivers would react to the police car with lights and sirens.

Often, communications would be updating us with new information about the call. But that night they had lost contact with the caller and couldn't get him back on the line. My colleague Barry contacted the second patrol car by radio to check that they were on their way, ready to give us security cover in case of a terrorist attack.

We arrived to find the house in darkness. Opening the heavy car doors, we burst out onto the street. Our gun belts rattled as we ran to the house. Barry kicked in the front door. It flew open, crashing against the wall with a loud bang. The hallway was in darkness but the street lights threw a glow onto the staircase. And, to my horror, I saw the outline of a man hanging from the bannister. My heart sank.

'He's still warm!' shouted Barry. 'Cut him down!' There was scant room to manoeuvre in the narrow hallway, but we managed to cut him free and lie him down. Without thinking, I tilted the man's head back and began blowing air into his mouth, while Barry started chest compression.

I could smell liquor on the man's breath as I blew. We silently willed him to live, but I sensed that we weren't going to win the fight. When the paramedics arrived and took over, they, too, failed to breathe life into him. Despite our best efforts, the man was dead.

The pain in my bottom brings me back to the present. It feels as if the bedpan is ripping the skin off me. Finally, a nurse comes running into the ward. She has tears in her eyes as she says, 'Right, Clodagh, let's get you off this bedpan.'

Was she feeling like I was only a few months ago? Had she been fighting to save a life – but lost the battle?

I feel safe during the night in RABIU. The compassion and kindness of the nurses amaze me. The night nurses make sure I'm comfortable, taking time to communicate with the spelling board. When they give me night-time medication and check my stats, they talk to me.

I always feel especially safe when Linda is on duty. Linda sits beside Mary and sings softly to her, gently rubbing her stomach to soothe her. I fall asleep to the gentle sound of her singing and, when I wake again, Linda is still there.

I spell this out to Adrian. I say how impressed I am with Linda.

'She has no agenda,' I spell. 'Her bosses don't know she is doing it. She gets no reward.' It's one of the kindest things I have ever seen anyone do.

I spell out the same to Linda. She thanks me, but says it's no big deal.

'I'm just doing my job, Clodagh. Nothing more.' That's how she sees it. I think she's an exceptionally good nurse. And she's not the only one. During my first few weeks in RABIU my shoulder drops and is unbearably sore. Several of the nurses rub it for me until I fall asleep. That kind of care amazes me.

Some nurses remain frightened of the spelling board. They might try it, but they say that technology scares them. It frightens me when they're on duty. If something's wrong, I won't be able to communicate to them what it is.

Mia, my night nurse, is determined to use the board.

'Let's talk, Clodagh. Are you comfortable?'

But she keeps holding the spelling board the wrong way and I can't blink at the letters. She hasn't a clue how to work it. I close my eyes tight. I want her to leave. Mia is frustrated and says, 'Why won't you do this with me?' Furious, I spit out, 'Fucking get me someone else!'

She stares at me, putting her hand in front of her mouth to hide the fact she is smiling.

'Clodagh, did you just say, "Fucking get me someone else?"'

And I did! I used the actual words. I'm amazed. We both start laughing. We laugh until we cry. When I stop laughing I realise this a huge development. I said an actual sentence. From now on I try harder to talk, rather than resorting to the spelling board. It's the only way my speech is going to get better. I practise and practise. Practise will surely make me sound more intelligible. The nurses work with me, listening, trying to understand. They are extraordinarily patient.

I practise in our rest period and in the evenings. Even though I'm not yet intelligible, I read with Diane. I practise obsessively and I'm still making noises when the night nurses come on duty. They laugh at me.

'You are allowed to take a break, Clodagh!' they say.

But I don't want to. I want to get better. And I am improving. Bronagh gives me more sounds to practise and exercises to strengthen my swallow. Every day we make sounds – 'k, k, k; ta ta ta; as, as, as'. We play a game where Bronagh has to guess the word I'm saying. She gets some of them right. I know that some day she will get every one right. I know that some day I will talk again.

The hospital arranges our first family meeting. Everyone has to be there – the team of doctors and nurses, all the therapists and the psychologist. Adrian and Diane are to attend as well. Before the meeting there is a pre-meeting so that everyone will have some idea what is up for discussion.

My case worker asks me, 'What are your goals in rehabilitation, Clodagh?'

I spell: 'I want to leave rehab walking and talking. I know I will be far from perfect.'

He looks perturbed.

'Clodagh, you do know what locked-in syndrome is?'

I nod.

'Then you understand you won't walk or talk. Your goals have to be realistic.'

I'm confused. Why am I having rehabilitation if I'm not going to walk and talk? I know that he's wrong – that I *will* walk. I *will* talk.

I spell out: 'You are full of bullshit.'

He looks impatient.

'Clodagh, you do know that what you say here has to go on your notes?'

What did he mean by goals? Surely walking and talking are goals?

I spell out: 'This place, and you, are full of bullshit.'

'Do you want me to record that?'

I blink once.

'If that's what you really want, Clodagh.'

When this is read out at the real meeting, Bronagh tries to stifle her laughter. But the doctors seem less impressed. Especially the psychologist.

'I'm worried about Clodagh's state of mind,' he says. This comment throws me. The psychologist performed tests with me when I was admitted to RABIU and he knows there is nothing wrong with my mind. 'She's too positive. And, as we all know, too much positivity can lead to disappointment.'

But I *have* to be positive. I have a choice – fight or give up. And I'm fighting. Taking every ounce of concentration, I manage to spit out the words, 'I will be the best I can be.'

And, for a minute, there is silence.

Then Adrian speaks.

'I don't think you understand,' he says. 'Clodagh isn't expecting a full recovery. She is telling you she will be the best she can be, whatever that is.

She is prepared to put in all the work, all the hours that will take.' He talks briefly about my work, about my fitness. 'Clodagh has more determination than anyone I have ever met. All she wants – all we, her family, want – is for all of you, her therapists, to work with her to make that happen.'

There is a lot of nodding, and the meeting ends on a more positive note.

I have to believe I will walk and talk again. I have never wanted anything more. I will do everything I can to make both of those things happen.

CHAPTER TWELVE

Adrian Will Have a Lesser Life

I agree to give the spelling board to another patient. The thought terrifies me, but I need to challenge myself. How will I manage when most people can't work out what I'm saying? Adrian tells me it's the right decision. And, although managing without the spelling board is frustrating, it has its positive side. Sure, there are people who can't understand me. KD finds it impossible. It drives both her and me mad. But Adrian and Diane manage fine. And that's the main thing.

The best thing is that my mum always knows exactly what I'm saying, straight away, even when Adrian is puzzled. She loves knowing that she can understand me better than Adrian or Diane.

'It must be because you were there when Clodagh learned to talk the first time,' says Adrian.

Whatever the reason, it makes me happy.

Each day, as I practise my sounds, I keep trying to lift my arms. I want to be able to raise them more than half a centimetre. I know that life would be easier if I could only move an arm. I want to feed myself, brush my own hair, clean my own teeth, wipe away my own tears. It would be wonderful just to be able to scratch an itch.

Then, at the end of May, I manage to lift my left hand and touch my nose. It has been less than two months since the stroke, but it has felt like a lifetime. I could burst with joy. My arm gets tired quickly. I ask Mum to bring me a magazine. I'm excited I will be able to read when I'm not in therapy. But I'm upset when my hand is too weak to turn the pages.

'I have an idea,' declares Diane.

The next night, at visiting time, she brings in a Kindle. I've never wanted one – I've always preferred reading actual books.

'Clodagh,' she says, 'you'll be able to manage this with one hand. It's so simple to operate.' She picks it up and shows me how to swipe the screen. And, although I need someone else to type in the password to start it, I manage to swipe the screen to turn pages. Reading is liberating.

The best thing is that the Kindle can access the internet. I don't bother with novels; I download all the books I can find about stroke and locked-in syndrome, and I start to read them aloud to practise my speech. Knowledge is power. I'm consumed with the need to know everything about stroke recovery.

Reading aloud is unbelievably hard. I can't breathe properly and I can only manage one word at a time. It doesn't even sound like reading – it's more like groaning. No one would understand that these noises are actually words, but I persevere. I read and I read. My Kindle is on my knee for every therapy session.

Siobhan, my neurophysio, asks me what I am reading every day. Every day I say, 'Stroke book.' Every day we laugh at this. I like Siobhan a lot. Whereas Bronagh is young and fun, Siobhan is mature and a real lady. She looks a lot like Helen Mirren.

Siobhan explains things to me in a way I like. She never tells me I am definitely going to get better, but she never tells me I'm not going to either. Instead she tells me to think of the milestones of a baby's development. Babies learn to sit, then to stand, then to take steps. Then they walk, I say to myself, and then they run! How I wish that day wasn't so far away!

Some days I wake and forget that the stroke has happened to me. I think about what route I'll take on my run today; but then I remember. I try to swing my legs out of bed, to get up and put on my running shorts and trainers. But my legs don't move, I can't sit up. I have to lie and watch the ceiling, waiting for a nurse to come get me dressed for the day and hoist me into a wheelchair.

My speech now is such that my family and medical staff can make it out, although it still takes patience and time on their part. I know in the world outside RABIU no one would understand me. I have no breath control and I can only manage one syllable per breath. My tongue tires easily and my lips can't form all the sounds. In particular, 'f', 'k' and 's' feel impossible. I like 'a', though. It's easy.

'I'd like one day away from stroke,' I tell Adrian. 'To go for a run and recharge so that I can fight it better.' But Adrian doesn't indulge my self-pity. He looks me in the eye and says, 'We will beat this. We *are* beating this.'

The trouble is, I'm not a patient person. I never have been – it's just not in my nature. I realise that this will be a long recovery. I'm a long way off going home, going back to work and running again. I *have* to believe that I will some day. At the same time, I have to accept that this is my life for now and enjoy my time in rehab.

I tell Adrian this and he looks surprised. I ask him to write on a whiteboard opposite my bed, 'Enjoy rehab – it's a strange, unexpected vacation. My aim: home to the Forever House.'

When Adrian finishes writing, I ask him to bring me photographs of the garden of our Forever House to stick on the board.

I must block my ears to anything negative. A young neurophysio asks me in the corridors one day whether my family have selected a nursing home for me. My social worker tells me I have to learn to accept that I will be spending the rest of my life in a wheelchair. She tells Adrian that my illness is difficult and that it's okay if he leaves me. No one will think any less of him.

All of this makes me smile, because I know I will prove them wrong. Adrian won't leave me. I will get my life back. I will return to work.

By June, my left arm, hand and fingers have gained strength. This makes a huge difference to me. It means I can lift a tumbler to my mouth and drink with a straw. I can press the nurse-call button with my hand. Occupational therapy arrive one day with an electric wheelchair. It's still big and ugly, but there's a crucial difference. I'll be able to operate it myself.

When I'm hoisted into it, I feel like a big kid with a go-kart. I can't stop laughing.

'Here are the controls,' says the therapist, telling me I might not be able to manage the joystick positioned on the armrest. I want to tell her that I'm used to driving armoured Land Rovers – whilst being petrol-bombed. But my speech won't allow it, so I take the joystick and drive across the ward. My hand gets tired, but it's only 30 seconds before I'm ready to go again. I'll be able to go where I want, when I want. This is happiness!

I have to concentrate, but I can press the button to open the ward door using my left arm. When Adrian arrives, we leave the ward and go to the canteen. I manoeuvre the chair up and down the corridor, laughing and laughing. I just can't stop! He laughs and laughs with me.

We sit in the canteen. Adrian drinks coffee and I drink thickened tea from a special cup. Then real life bursts my rehab bubble. Adrian tells me he needs to sell my car. I'm shocked. Does he believe I'll never drive again? Is he losing faith that I will recover?

Denying this, he says, 'Think about it, Clodagh. The car is sitting at the house, not being driven, depreciating in value. And we need the money.'

I see his logic but, even so, it's like a punch in the gut. I cry.

'As soon as you can drive again, you can have whatever car you want,' he says, and I nod.

When Sister Malone tells me that I'm moving to my own room, I feel nervous. I like being in the ward. Talking to Lisa and Lesley helps pass the time. We always have a laugh and there's a lot going on.

'It makes sense, Clodagh,' she says. 'You're one of our long-term patients.'

I hate being reminded of that.

When I tell Adrian I'm being moved, he laughs.

'They're trying to get rid of you,' he says. I look at him sharply. 'You can be a right pain, you know. It's like you're conducting a patrol, but instead of it being at work, it's in the rehab unit.'

Sister Malone leads me to the room. I follow in the electric wheelchair.

'Look, Clodagh,' she says. 'You've got a view of the garden.' There are baskets of flowers hanging from trees just outside the window. She tells me that Wilnor hung them there especially for me.

Wilnor is one of my favourite therapists. He refuses to use the spelling board.

'You and I will talk to each other, Clodagh, no matter how long it takes,' he says.

One day, when I'm finding life particularly tough, Wilnor tells me, 'Clodagh, you are like a caterpillar. You think your world has ended but you're just in your cocoon. Soon you will become a butterfly. You will spread your wings and fly.'

Being unable to control my outward emotions, this made me howl and howl with happiness. But Wilnor understood, and he laughed.

I ask Adrian to hang up the pictures that were once strung over my head in the stroke ward, and he does. I need them – pictures of the flowers we planted in the garden, of the hot tub and of our kitchen, where we danced. There are pictures of our travels. Will I ever be able to go on a plane again? There's a picture of me skydiving in Namibia. That picture is important to me because the memory of it once kept me alive. I stare at the pictures every day as I do my speech exercises. I tell myself I will be home before Christmas.

I still dream about the skydive. About the wind rushing against my face. I imagine I'm breathing the air deep, deep into my lungs. Now I wake full of hope. I can wipe away my own tears and brush my own hair. I'm beginning to be able to brush my own teeth. I can say good morning. I look forward to the challenge of every day. One day I will skydive again. I know it.

When Adrian visits, I wheel myself out of the unit. We both like visiting the canteen and the garden. Adrian has returned to work and he brings me messages from my colleagues. I love hearing from them, but it upsets me too. They're getting ready for the marching season, when trouble often flares between the two communities here. My new job with the Tactical Support Group would be starting now. I'd be out, patrolling the streets, keeping people safe. Now I'm sitting in a wheelchair, wearing a nappy.

'It's so hard trying to stay positive,' I say, and Adrian can see how much I'm struggling. He suggests that we get out for the day. All my therapists agree that it's a good idea.

Adrian suggests going into Belfast, to the university area, where we can get lunch and go to the cinema. Adrian works out how to get a train. Diane brings me the clothes I've asked her to pick up and, after applying make-up with my shaky left hand, I look like myself again. As I look at my reflection I feel happy. I am wearing pink chinos that fit comfortably over my nappy; my hair has been cut short and is no longer askew; the red scar from my tracheostomy is fading. I don't look ill.

It's a beautiful day. Adrian wheels me towards the train station, away from the hospital. We both grin. It feels wonderful, like we have escaped. We take the train to the university area. But, as he pushes me along the streets, my legs go into spasm and keep slipping off the footrest. It's annoying. Smiling, Adrian says, 'I can fix that,' and he leaves me for a moment outside a haberdashery shop.

I lift my head to the sun and take in the sounds of the city. Then Adrian emerges with a paper bag. Delighted with himself, he picks up my feet and sticks Velcro onto the soles of my sandals and onto the footplate. It works! My feet stay put.

I expect everyone to stare at us – especially when Adrian has to straighten me up in the wheelchair. I have no core control so I fall to the side without help. But they don't. And, as we sit in Starbucks drinking coffee, mine with added thickener from the tub we've brought with us from the unit, I feel utterly content.

On our way to the cinema we see a former inspector of mine from work.

'Run!' I tell Adrian.

'Why?' he asks.

'Self-preservation. I don't want him to hear my speech.'

Laughing, he pushes me as fast as he can and runs all the way to the cinema.

'This is ridiculous,' he says, and we both laugh at our juvenile behaviour.

I wouldn't normally have chosen to see this particular film, but it doesn't matter. I am a woman going out with her boyfriend. That is enough. The movie makes me laugh, and once I start I just can't stop. This sets Adrian off too. It does me so much good.

As Adrian wheels me back to RABIU, he says, 'You know something? I know you're going to get better, but if you didn't – if you were in a wheelchair for life – it wouldn't matter. We would cope – and we could still have fun!'

I feel happy hearing him say that, because I had worried that pushing me around would be too much for him.

'Do you mean that?'

'As long as we can communicate – and laugh together – we can cope with anything,' he says.

I love you, I think to myself. I go back into RABIU feeling really happy.

But when I wake the next morning, my happiness has evaporated. I hate this place. The nurses' laughter fills the corridors. I hate them because they're happy. I hate the rattle of the drugs trolley as it rolls towards my room every day. I hate what has happened to me. I can't bear it.

I hear someone enter my room. I lie still, pretending to be asleep in the hope that they'll leave me alone. But a hand rests on my arm, my occupational therapist says my name and, when I open my eyes, asks if I'd like a shower.

'We'll wheel you in on the Stedy rather than transferring you to and from the wheelchair,' she says. Inwardly I groan. The Stedy, a contraption like a walking frame on wheels, was introduced to me a few days ago. There's a seat attached that folds down. To use it you need strength in your arms as well as your legs, and some control of your core muscles. I find it a huge challenge.

I wish I could take myself to the bathroom. I hate having no privacy and relying on the nurses to wash me and dress me. Sometimes they put my hand splints on wrong; sometimes they tie my shoes too tight.

The therapist wheels me into the bathroom on the Stedy and carefully positions it at the toilet, so I can use it with the help of the rails. As I sit there, she goes and gathers my clothes for the day. I hear a nurse asking if I'm ready for my meds. Someone else asks how long I'll be in there. She needs to take my blood to check my warfarin levels.

Yesterday seems like a distant dream.

The therapist begins by mentioning the cinema trip as she enters with my clothes. Then she says, 'It's good of Adrian to accept a lesser life.'

I stare at her, appalled. Adrian won't have a lesser life just because I am in a wheelchair – for now. Why would he? We can still communicate, laugh and love. Our life is different from what *she* thinks is normal. Different isn't lesser!

I'm furious with her. Especially because she made her statement when I'm sitting on the toilet, unable to get up, and my adult nappy is lying on the floor beside me. The frustrating thing is that, as much as I want to challenge her, I can't, because my speech is still so awful. Tears sting my eyes.

Worse still, I need her now. She helps me transfer to the Stedy and onto an ugly, bulky shower chair. Where once showers were a pleasure for me, now they are a necessary evil. I don't feel safe. When I get wet, I'm terrified I'll slip off the chair and, when I lean forward to wash my legs, I'm worried I'll topple and hit my head on the ground.

For all that, the chair is a step up from what the nurses called the 'duck pond'. When I first arrived in RABIU and had no mobility, they would roll me onto a narrow plastic trolley, take me to the bathroom on it and strip me naked. I'd lie on the trolley, motionless, as two nurses would hose my body down and wash my hair.

I make myself a promise. Not only will I be the best I can be, I will also make sure that Adrian never has a lesser life. It won't happen. I won't let it.

Now that Lisa and I are no longer in the same ward, meeting her at mealtimes becomes more important to me. We take tea together and stay behind in the canteen once dinner is over. She is patient. My speech and swallow are much better now, but my voice still tires easily.

When there isn't space to manoeuvre my chair next to Lisa, it bothers me. It's hard sitting beside someone whose evening meal is peg-fed into their stomach. Or someone who feeds themselves but can't talk, or someone who doesn't want to talk to me, Chewbacca.

One night another patient shouts at me for being too happy.

'Look at you, all happy, happy in your wheelchair! Someone of us want to walk again.'

I smile at her. I say nothing, but I think, *I don't just want to walk again, I want to run again. And I will. And why should I not be happy until that day comes?*

As I leave the dining room that day, Peter, the deputy sister, asks, 'Is everything okay?' He has noticed the tension at our dinner table. I tell him I find the dining room difficult at times, for different reasons. It is hard watching people whose life has been torn apart by brain injury, just like me, in the blink of an eye. I admire the nurses who, every night, spoon-feed patients, talk to them, laugh with them – who treat everyone as though they are perfectly normal. I know I couldn't do their job. They have such kind hearts.

Peter thinks for a minute.

'Clodagh, why don't you get Adrian to take you out for dinner?'

I look at him and smile.

'Would that be okay?'

'Provided you get your meds and tell someone you're going.'

As soon as I reach my room I message Adrian from my laptop and tell him. I can type now. It is painstakingly slow, because I have no movement in my right arm and very limited power in my left. I was right handed before the stroke. My left arm fatigues easily and my fingers stiffen with little movement, but I find it liberating to be able to type anything. I send messages to Adrian and my mum. They often contain just one word – 'Hello' – but it makes me ecstatic to be able to compose them. They reply with long messages that are equally joyful.

Adrian replies at once: 'Excellent.' He suggests we find a nice restaurant on the Lisburn Road, a short walk from the hospital. He sounds as happy as I am.

Next, I message Diane, asking her to come in with Mum in the afternoon to help me get ready. When she agrees, I think, not only do I have the best partner in the world, I have the best sister too.

The following afternoon, Diane and Mum carefully manoeuvre me into the shower chair. We don't know if Diane is really allowed to shower me but, now I have my own room – and it has its own bathroom – she showers me most evenings. When she arrives, she bursts into my room, saying, 'Let's get illegal shower time started!' I have missed showering every day. I love the way she washes my hair. When she and Mum have towelled me dry, she even gets a hair-dryer and dries my hair.

Today she shaves my legs, dresses me in a pretty dress she has collected from my house and helps with my make-up. My hair is glossy and, wearing perfume, I feel feminine. When Adrian arrives and tells me I look beautiful, I almost believe him.

It's a beautiful summer evening. Adrian wheels me down the Lisburn Road in Belfast. We have a wonderful meal. So what if my feet have to be strapped to the wheelchair with Velcro? Who cares that I have a nappy on underneath my dress? And if I can't talk properly, and can barely sit up, what does any of that matter? Adrian has to cut up my food for me. We add a little thickener to the wine, but it feels acidic on my throat and the taste is too strong. So we water it down a little. It really isn't pleasurable to drink, but I can hardly believe I am having a glass of wine with my dinner after everything. I'm eating macaroons for dessert. It all feels normal. If this is what it takes to get me out to dinner, well, that's fine by me!

As Adrian pays the bill and wheels me back to RABIU, I sigh with contentment. Life isn't lesser, I think. It's just different.

CHAPTER THIRTEEN

A Visit to the Seaside

The great thing about being in RABIU is that it makes me forget, at times, just how disabled I am. I am making progress and, although it feels painstakingly slow, being able to use my left arm to change TV channels and eat by myself makes me so very happy. Adrian mentions that, when I am discharged from hospital, he will take three months off work, but I can't figure out why.

'Why do you think? To look after you, of course.'

I can't get my head around that. Surely, once I get out of hospital, I'll be able to look after myself? Isn't that why I'm in RABIU?

'Don't you think I'm going to get well again?' I say. 'Don't you see how hard I'm working?'

Adrian just looks at me. He colours, but doesn't say a word. 'Well, don't you?'

He still doesn't answer, and I get a lump in my throat. He puts his arms around me and I cry uncontrollably.

'You *will* get well. I know you are working hard,' he says. 'But, Clodagh, it might take a little longer than you think.'

Breathlessly, between sobs, I manage to say, 'I should be at work *now*. Especially now that it's the marching season.' He holds my hand. 'I'll never drive an armoured Land Rover again. That breaks my heart.'

Adrian laughs. Then he shakes me, gently.

'Stop romanticising, Clodagh.'

'Romanticising?'

'Stop saying how great it was. You were always complaining!' I join in with his laughter. 'Remember? You complained all the time.'

And I had to concede his point.

'I guess you're right. I did moan a lot when I was detailed driver for a 12-hour shift.'

'Exactly!' He throws his arms in the air. '*Now* you remember! Clodagh, you might need a different role when you return, but it's possible that you'll like it.'

I bury my head in his chest.

'It's going to be okay, isn't it?'

'Yes, it is! More than okay. And, meanwhile, you have to concentrate on your therapies. After that, we'll plan our next adventure!'

Adrian is taking me out to dinner again. I'm waiting for Lynsey, one of my favourite nurses, to help me to get ready when my cousin Erin appears. I haven't seen her since my stroke and she has arrived when visiting time is over. I'm glad to see her, but Adrian is collecting me in half an hour and I need to get ready. I try to explain this to Erin.

'I'm sorry, Erin, but I really need to get ready to go out with Adrian.'

There's pity in her eyes. And panic.

'I'm sorry,' she says, handing me a magazine, 'but I can't understand you.'

I'm disappointed she doesn't understand me. I thought my speech was becoming more intelligible with all those hours of practice. I repeat the sentence, in my best Chewbacca voice, more slowly and deliberately, and finally she understands. Or, at least, she says she does. 'That's what I thought you said.'

She doesn't elaborate, but from the way she stares at me it's clear that she still hasn't got it. I guess she doesn't want to offend me by asking to repeat myself again.

Lynsey arrives and says, 'Right, Clodagh. What are you wearing for date night?'

'Date night?' Erin says to Lynsey, sounding confused but smiling. 'So I did understand you after all, Clodagh!'

I speak to Lynsey, confident Erin won't understand me.

'My cousin thinks I have lost it. But I'm not waiting until I recover fully to start living my life again.' Lynsey laughs.

'Your cousin is very demanding,' she says to Erin. 'She rules this place, you know! We are like her assistants in here. I'm helping her put on a dress tonight because she is going out for dinner with Adrian.'

'Okay,' says Erin. Her expression tells me she's still not sure this isn't some trick by the nurses to keep their patient happy. 'I'll leave you to get ready.'

Erin kisses my cheek before leaving my room. Lynsey laughs.

'I don't think she really believes you're going out for dinner.'

'No, I don't think she does.'

We both laugh. Erin's confusion over the whole dinner date is funny, but something about it makes a sick feeling fill my stomach. It's a sharp reminder that, although I've accepted my disabilities and I'm working hard to overcome them, there are people who will find the change in me shocking and difficult to accept.

I know everyone thinks I will never be able to talk or walk – and I admit to myself that it's true that I'm a long way away from being able to do either. Will Adrian keep believing me when I tell him I'm going to keep working at this? Will he believe me when I say I know I will walk again? Or will he see the doubt that everyone else has and walk away from me?

My family are on holiday in Portrush for a week. Usually I take a few days' leave from work and go with them. I love it there. With the long beaches and sea air I forget all about work. The big kid in me loves swimming in the sea and going on the rattly rollercoaster at Barry's amusement's. It's breaking my heart that this year I can't be with them.

The next day, during therapy, it plays on my mind. As Bronagh and I sit in the garden, doing speech exercises, I'm imagining my family walking along the beach. When Wilnor is helping me exercise my right hand, I'm thinking the same. By the time I get to Siobhan for physiotherapy, I've formulated a plan in my mind. I've decided – I am going to visit my family in Portrush.

We're practising my sitting balance when I say it.

'Can I go to Portrush?'

'Portrush?' Standing back, Siobhan looks me in the eye. 'How would you get there?'

'Train,' I say, keeping it short, because I'm tired and my speech is laboured. Siobhan keeps it short, too.

'No,' she says, and I know it's pointless to argue with her. But I don't give up on the idea. I mention it to the nurses when I return to the ward. They look at each other, and then look at me.

'Portrush? But Clodagh, you're not even continent – your catheter has only just been removed.'

I'm still not defeated. I tell Adrian my great idea. And he agrees at once.

'Portrush? Why not? We could go for the day. Sounds great!'

I love the fact that Adrian doesn't think it's a foolish idea. I love the fact that he hasn't said it's impossible. After all, I know that he's the one who will have to help me make it happen. Mum, Dad and Diane are beginning to get used to the wheelchair, but manoeuvring me onto a train would still be too difficult for them. Adrian is a problem solver. He likes proving people wrong.

'But everyone I have mentioned it to has said no.'

'Have you asked Dr McCann?'

I shake my head.

'Who do you go to in work when you have something important to ask?'

'The boss?'

'Exactly!'

'You're right,' I say.

When I see Dr McCann in the corridor of the unit, I seize the opportunity.

Dr McCann is the senior consultant in RABIU. He's an older man, maybe in his sixties, with thinning grey hair. He looks distinguished, always wearing a bow tie and glasses. I can tell that all the staff respect him. He greets me with a smile.

'Hello, Clodagh.'

I ask him at once if I can go to Portrush. He plays with his bow tie.

'Why do you want to go there?'

'Because I nearly died. Because I'm alive. Because I want to see the sea, and my family are there.'

'Yes, that's okay,' he says. I could squeal with happiness.

I hear him announce the news at the nurses' station.

'Clodagh wants to go to the seaside,' he says. 'Let's make it possible.'

'Are you joking?' asks Bonnie, one of the nurses.

'I am a consultant,' he says. 'I don't do jokes.'

I imagine him smiling as he strides along the corridor. Bonnie comes into my room, laughing.

'My goodness, Clodagh,' she says. 'You always get whatever you want!'

I'm ecstatic, but not everyone is happy. The nurses keep repeating their concerns about my incontinence. They fear it will set back my adult potty training. The occupational therapist is concerned that I won't manage the toilet without a Stedy, and everyone else thinks it's a crazy idea because I need too much care.

'How will Adrian cope for a whole day?' asks Lynsey.

I feel sure that my occupational therapist wants to thwart the whole trip. And it's not until I agree to bring Adrian in so she can teach him to use a bedpan that she relents. Adrian agrees to come in and be trained, but the whole thing feels ridiculous. I have no intention of using a bedpan with Adrian. I will wear an adult nappy all day.

I go along with the charade so that the trip happens. I want to see the sea and smell the salt air so badly. The stillness of the air inside the hospital only reminds me how little I can move. I desperately want to feel the wind in my face. I'd love it to rain. I'd be thrilled to feel heavy, wet raindrops on my face. I'd be thrilled to feel anything that would make me forget the stillness of my body, forget that nothing really moves.

I tell Adrian that if he places me on the bedpan just this once, he will never ever have to do it again. I need this trip – and I'm prepared to tolerate any amount of embarrassment to make it happen.

The day comes. On the train, I remind him that I'm wearing an adult nappy and will not drink anything until I get back to RABIU. He laughs.

'Listen, it's only a big deal if you make it a big deal. We'll sort out what needs sorted out. Now, forget about all that and let's enjoy our escape!'

'OK. Can I sit on a normal seat and not the wheelchair?' Adrian smiles and lifts me from the wheelchair onto a seat. I keep falling sideways because I still have no control over my core. Adrian pushes me up, checking I'm comfortable. He tries to straighten me when I fall onto his shoulder but I say, 'No, leave me.'

I am so happy. As I sit there, looking out of the window, absorbing all I can see, I feel alive and I can't stop smiling. When the train arrives in Portrush my heart pounds with excitement. I can't wait to surprise my family. But most of all I can't wait to breathe in the sea air.

Adrian wheels me along the seafront to my family's house, a mile from the station. The weather is perfect. It's a grey day. There is drizzle on my face, on my hands, on my feet. I'm wearing sandals. There's a cold wind blowing in my face, surfers are riding the waves and seagulls are cawing. For the first time in four months, I feel truly alive.

All the family are at the house, gathered for a barbecue, not expecting me to arrive. Only Diane is in on the surprise. She has organised everything. We've texted her, saying we're almost there, and she's left the door on the latch.

My heart thuds with excitement. Adrian wheels me into kitchen, which is full of laughter. It falls dead silent when everyone catches sight of me. Then Mum, sounding shocked, laughs, 'Clodagh! I can't believe it! How did you get here?'

Dad, laughing too, kisses my forehead. He doesn't talk but has a huge grin. Everyone cries. Emily nudges my arm and whispers that she, Adam and Hannah were in on the secret too – and kept it. Diane brought them all to the hospital the previous day to make sure there wouldn't be a repeat of the Hannah incident in the stroke ward. Their first visit was a success. I cried when I first saw them but Diane had prepared them well, telling them, 'Aunty Clodagh might cry when she first sees you – but that just means she is happy.'

I haven't seen most of the family since I became ill, because I've been restricting visitors – for their sake as much as mine. It's not easy visiting someone who can't talk properly. It feels surreal to be in a room with them all now. I love listening to them chatter.

We stay for an hour, eating Diane's barbecue food. My swallow has progressed and I can now manage food of normal consistency, even though it has to be in small bitesize pieces and I have to chew them well. Chewing is exhausting because my mouth muscles are weak, but still, food is a pleasure. Diane cuts up my food like a parent does for her baby. She positions my wheelchair so that the table is on my left and sets a plate on the table. She smiles as she walks away. I can feed myself now but my arm tires easily. Diane has set me up so that I can rest my arm on the table whenever I need to.

I listen to everyone's chatter, I watch as they walk around the room. My heart could burst as it surges with love for all the people in the room. I look at the clock, I know it is time to leave. I say to Adrian, 'Can we go to the beach and get ice cream?'

He laughs. I can see in his face this has been as good for him as it has been for me. 'Of course. If that's what you want to do, that's what we'll do.'

Everyone comes out to the front of the house to wave me goodbye. There are hugs, laughter and tears. I am so happy Adrian and Diane have helped me pull off the surprise.

'I need to get some rock,' I say to Adrian, as he pushes my wheelchair back in the direction of the seafront.

'Rock?'

'For the nurses. I want to give them something with "Portrush" on it. It will prove that I've been here.' I hope, too, that the rock will make them realise that nothing is impossible. All the problems they listed have had solutions. No matter how bad a patient seems, with love and support, they can do much more than they might expect.

I am tired on the journey home. Tired, but very, very happy. Adrian holds my hand and chats to me as I struggle to keep my eyes open.

'I'm proud of you, Clodagh,' he says. 'I told you we could do this. There is nothing we can't do.'

I feel victorious when Adrian wheels me into the ward. I know I look dishevelled. The wind has rumpled my short hair. I can feel warmth rush to my face as we leave the night air behind us. I feel victorious when Adrian wheels me into the ward, which is buzzing softly as the nurses get the patients ready for bed.

'And the wanderer returns!' says a nurse, catching sight of us. She looks me up and down to check I'm still in one piece. 'I hope you've brought us some rock!'

Adrian hands her a bag. She laughs, and says, 'I was only joking, but thank you very much! I'll enjoy this.' She waves the bag at the nurses' station as if she is weaving a magic spell. The other nurses come running to collect their own stick of rock.

'You did it! We knew you would!'

I smile, but I am well aware that I could never have done this alone. Without everyone's help, today would not have been possible. The stick of rock is my way of saying thank you.

It's the end of July, and the plan is to get me home for the weekend. I'll be allowed to go as soon as I can make car transfers. I practise obsessively during rest times. I wheel myself into the bathroom and, using the towel rail, pull myself to my feet. I stand from the wheelchair and sit down again. I keep this up for hours. Whenever I get tired I take a short rest, then start again. I will do anything if it means I can go home.

When the consultant and all my therapists agree I'm ready, Adrian comes in for a car-transfer test. He has to prove that he can help me manoeuvre myself from the wheelchair to the passenger seat of the car. I warn him to lift me if my legs prove too weak, but to do so in a way that won't be noticed. I desperately want to go home to the Forever House.

On the day of the test, Adrian's eyes are bloodshot with tiredness, because he has just worked a night shift. He should really be in bed to get some sleep before going back on duty tonight, but he knows how much I want to go home.

Somehow, despite my weak, shaky legs, we pass.

'That's great,' says Lynsey. 'Now we need to get your house equipped.'

Confused, Adrian and I look at each other, then at Lynsey.

'Equipped?'

'You need a commode,' she says, 'a Stedy and a hospital bed.'

'I'm not using a hospital bed at home.' She looks at me and narrows her eyes, but remains silent. 'When I go home I'm going to lie in my own bed.'

Adrian squeezes my shoulder. I know that he means by the squeeze: listen to her!

'Clodagh, I know that's what you want. But you're not used to an ordinary bed any more. You've been sleeping on an adjustable electric bed – you can move your mattress until you're completely comfortable. I really don't think you'll manage without it.'

'I've been practising,' I say.

And so I have. I've been sleeping flat in my hospital bed because I'm determined to sleep in my own bed. I don't argue the point, though. They can deliver the bed – but I have no intention of sleeping in it.

I wake full of nervous excitement for that first weekend. Will Adrian have kept the house clean? Will the plants have grown in the garden? Will we manage the Stedy?

Adrian arrives, Caoimhe smiling beside him. We turn to go.

'Hang on there a minute,' says a nurse. 'We've got to go through everything with Adrian.'

They give him complicated instructions, making sure he knows all about my meds, telling him how important it is that I get them at the right time. Then they ask if he has any worries or questions. Is he happy that he can manage?

I am becoming impatient. I want to go!

'Okay,' they say, after what feels like an age. 'You're free to go!'

Pushing my wheelchair, Adrian breaks into a run.

'Let's escape,' he says, 'before they change their minds!'

As we speed towards the car, laughing, I'm so happy I could explode. But I'm tired and weak from the day's therapies and I struggle to stand. Putting his arms round me, Adrian uses all his strength to help me manoeuvre into the car. I'm out of breath and I hit my head on the car door frame, but I don't care. I'm going home!

I sit, slumped like a rag doll, in the front passenger seat. Everything feels wrong. Adrian's car was never this uncomfortable before. I can't shift my body to get comfortable. But I stay quiet. I don't want to start the weekend by complaining. Putting the car into gear, Adrian drives off carefully. It takes all my efforts to stay upright. My face suddenly feels intensely hot. I begin to sweat. The minute he hits the main road, my head starts to spin. I can't seem to get used to the movement of the car. The hedges are rushing by and my eyes can't adjust. I feel faint. And I have a horrible feeling that I might throw up.

'Can you slow down? I'm sorry! I feel sick.'

Adrian glances at me and moves into the slow lane. He's crawling along.

'Are you okay? Do you think you'll make it home?'

'Yes. I just need to focus on the road.'

After a while, my brain starts to adjust to the car's motion. Even so, it's a huge relief when we stop and drop Caoimhe off at her grandfather's house. He comes out, gives me a hug and says, 'You're doing good, girl.' I smile, and manage, somehow, not to sob.

When we get to the outskirts of my home town and drive past the boutique that stocked the dress I wanted for Fiona's wedding, I start to cry. When Adrian buzzes us through the gates of the Forever House I cry louder. Adrian looks at me and laughs.

'We knew this was going to happen. Happy cries?' he asks as the car sweeps down the drive.

Transferring from the car to the wheelchair is a struggle. I'm physically weak and my mixture of laughing and crying isn't helping. But we manage, eventually, and he wheels me into the Forever House. Adrian lifts me gently onto the sofa, propping me up with a mountain of cushions, adjusting them under my knees and my bad arm. I am home! It feels a little like coming home after a long holiday – everything is as you left it but it still feels different. It smells different, too. Adrian hasn't been lighting scented candles like I do. But it looks clean and tidy. Half of me is happy at that; the other half is disappointed that Adrian has been coping fine without me.

I'm only home for three days, but I am deliriously happy, because next weekend I will be home for another three days.

We have a quiet evening on the sofa. I cry every so often and Adrian laughs. 'Happy?'

'I just can't believe I'm home,' I say. 'Part of me worried I would end up in a nursing home.'

On Saturday morning we laze about. Adrian wheels me around inside the house and outside – just to see that our home is as I left it. When Adrian tells me how empty the place felt without me, I am relieved and happy. Relieved that he needs me and happy that he missed me.

On Saturday evening Adrian wants to take me out and Diane has agreed to do my hair. She arrives after lunch, and a bit later Mum pops in.

'I've bought you something new to wear for tonight,' she says, presenting me with loose navy trousers and a pretty white top. 'Diane picked it. She said you'd love the trousers. You love navy.'

I love my mum. She's so good to me. I know she finds my illness difficult to understand and I'm scared that the worry will make her ill. I smile and tell her thank you and that she's the best.

'Where are you going?' Diane asks as she carefully plaits my hair.

'Our favourite restaurant,' I say.

On our way there I begin to feel nerves flutter in my stomach and thoughts race around in my head. They know me in that restaurant. What will they think of me now that I can't talk and that I'm falling over in a wheelchair? What if I see somebody I know? Will they want to talk to me? I know they won't be able to understand me. I know they'll be shocked. I'm just not ready for that.

I'm about to shout, 'I can't do this!' when Adrian, sensing my apprehension, says, 'It'll be fine, Clodagh.' When he parks the car and helps me into the wheelchair I feel as if I feel as if I might spontaneously combust. I've let my head fill with too many 'what if?' questions.

The manager, Adam, comes to greet us, just as he always does, and I watch his face anxiously. How is he going to react?

'Hi guys. Your usual table?'

It's as if nothing has changed. He doesn't say, 'You've cut your hair,' or, 'You are lopsided.' He doesn't mention the wheelchair. It's as if nothing has happened.

There's no hint of difference in his expression – not a flicker, of shock, dismay or revulsion. And there's no fuss. He whisks away the normal chair discreetly to make space for my wheelchair and hands me the menu with a smile, just like always. He treats me in exactly the way he always has, and I love him for it.

We're reading the menu when I recognise a woman at the table beside ours. It's someone I was at school with, although we weren't in the same year group. I wonder if she's seen me, and pray she hasn't.

We're eating our desserts when she gets up to leave. Approaching our table, she smiles.

'Clodagh,' she says, 'it's wonderful to see you looking so well.' There is such warmth in her voice, I know she means it. I thank her and explain this is my first weekend home. I spit every word out, concentrating hard on sounding every word correctly so that she understands me. 'Congratulations,' she says. 'I can tell you've been working really hard on your recovery. You're an inspiration. Really, you are.'

'That was nice,' says Adrian as the couple leave. 'I told you not to worry. Are you okay?'

I nod my head and fill with relief. 'How could I not be? She was so lovely!'

Back home, we snuggle together on the sofa like any normal couple, have a glass of wine – mine still watered down – and watch a movie. When it's over, Adrian says, 'You need your meds.'

I groan inwardly. He's talking about my nightly enema. I have been trying not to think about that part of the weekend.

'Sorry,' I say, my voice breaking. Adrian lifts me off the sofa, transfers me to the Stedy and wheels me along the hall to the bathroom. I sob loudly, unable to control my sobs. I hate what this illness has done to me. I hate the indignity of it. I hate the fact that Adrian is now my carer.

When I'm safely on the toilet, Adrian says in a stern voice, 'Clodagh, stop. This is just a moment in time. It's only a big deal if you make it a big deal. Okay?'

The whole ordeal completed, he dresses me for bed and wheels me to our bedroom on the Stedy. I avoid his eye, because I can't forget the horror of what has just happened, but when he climbs in beside me, moulding his body to mine, I allow myself to forget and enjoy the moment.

It is wonderful to sleep beside Adrian, to feel him next to me, not to be alone. I have missed my home, I have missed my bed and I have missed Adrian. I relax. With Adrian's arms around me, the nightmare of the early days of intensive care feels unreal. I sleep better than I've slept for months.

Another thing I have missed is Sunday brunch. When we were both off duty together it was one of our greatest pleasures. We'd get up late and Adrian would cook his runny poached eggs on toast. We'd eat them in front of *Sunday Brunch* on television.

Today, eggs have never tasted so good. We linger over a pot of coffee and I don't want this brunch to end.

When it finally does, Adrian showers me and dresses me. That's hard, because the bathroom is not adapted to my new needs. He has to lift me into the shower, sit me on an old kitchen stool and support me with one hand, because my core is so weak, while he washes my body and shampoos my hair. I'm not supposed to shower, just to wash over a sink. But I want to shower and, whatever I want, Adrian is making it happen. It's complicated, but he makes it seem effortless.

Sunday evening comes too quickly and I have to go back to RABIU. I cry as Adrian manoeuvres me into the car. This time my tears are not happy ones.

'Don't worry, Clodagh,' he says. 'You'll be back at home again next weekend. And the one after.'

He is as good as his word. Every weekend after that first one I go home. And every weekend Adrian takes me out for lunch, coffee or dinner. I'm happy. I do rehab during the week and I'm released for wonderful weekends.

Not every weekend is wonderful, though. The weekend I have my period is one of those. I don't know how to tell him. I'm quiet when he collects me, but when we're on the motorway I blurt it out.

His face doesn't change and for a moment I wonder if he has understood me.

'That's good, isn't it?' he says eventually. 'I remember how happy you were when your periods came back, that first week in rehab. This shows that your body is getting back to normal, right?'

I nod.

'But I need help in the bathroom.'

Adrian stares at the road.

'Well, that's okay,' he says. 'Remember, it's only a moment in time.'

I cry. Adrian puts his hand on my thigh and gives it a squeeze.

'Don't make a big deal of this, Clodagh. Just don't.'

I hate how helpless I am. Every ounce of my dignity gone. I have no secrets any more. Adrian fell in love with GI Jane, and now she is sitting, lopsided, in tears beside him in the car. Why does he stay?

Turning, Adrian glances at me.

'I can turn my emotions off,' he says. 'You know that, Clodagh. It's just the same for you. It's a skill you've developed at work. You have to. You just get on with things and then you leave them behind.'

He's right. A memory bubbles up and I start to laugh.

'What is it?' he asks.

'I'm thinking of that Saturday, a late shift in the custody suite, when you called me in and I thought you were making me a cup of tea.'

That was something Adrian did on the rare occasions when our shifts coincided. We'd chat for a while, just enjoying ten minutes together. But one day, instead of handing me a polystyrene cup, he told me he needed me to search a prisoner.

Adrian laughs. 'The woman who was hiding drugs?'

'Yes!' I say, remembering walking into a cell and being faced with a middle-aged woman in her underwear, falling out of a stained vest top. She stank of cigarettes and alcohol. Adrian told me that, when he informed her that she would have to remove her shoes, belt and any cords before she entered a cell, the lady had got angry and removed the few clothes she was wearing.

'It was not funny!' I say. 'I still haven't forgiven you! When I was searching around her groin area she bloody peed on me!'

'*She* found it funny,' laughs Adrian.

'Hilarious! It made everyone's night – except for mine.'

'But I did make you tea afterwards, remember? And you did find some drugs on her.'

I smile. Adrian always knows how to make me feel better.

CHAPTER FOURTEEN

The Two Pauls

It's early August and Lisa is going home. She is eight months pregnant and is to have her baby early, by caesarean section. She is excited – the baby is healthy, despite everything. I'm happy for her, but heartbroken to see her go. She has become my one great friend in RABIU.

I visit Lisa's room to say goodbye, but we can't say anything to each other, as we're both crying. Our bulky wheelchairs and one functioning arm each make giving each other a hug impossible. We simply hold hands, crying until we stop.

'I'll come visit after the baby is born,' promises Lisa. 'I'll bring him or her with me.'

'I will love that. Everyone will love that.'

Without Lisa, RABIU is harder. I miss her and the closeness we had. I'm surrounded by people every day, but I feel alone. I find myself living for my weekends at home.

I begin to worry that I'm not making progress and it's getting me down. I'm exhausted. I want to give up. Adrian and Diane don't help. When I complain about my condition, they dismiss my frustration and tell me I'm doing well. Yet *they* are always complaining too. Diane goes on about the traffic; Adrian bends my ear with his work problems. I just wish *I* could drive and work, but they don't get it. I wish they could spend a day as me. Then they'd understand.

I realise, too, that all the encouragement in the world won't make me better. I have to throw all my energy into my therapies. But I have lost my energy. Fighting this illness every day has exhausted me.

Fiona and Damien visit and mention a national trainee-investigators' exam at work. I start to get excited. This could help me find a role when I return to work – because I *will* return to work.

I tell Adrian I want to apply to sit the exam. I think it's a wonderful idea. Adrian laughs when I tell him. He says, 'I guess I'll be the one who needs to get it sorted.'

I get permission from my bosses, and from my consultant, to sit the exam. I wait, impatiently, for Adrian to bring in the manual I need. I'm keen to start studying. When Adrian arrives with it, I'm surprised at how big it is – and the amount of information I need to take in. But I don't let that deter me.

It's August now and we get some beautiful sunny days. I sit in the hospital garden under a magnificent tree, which has become my favourite place in RABIU. The manual sits awkwardly on my knees as I read it. Since Lisa has been discharged, I've found a new friend in a man I've named Silent Paul. He comes in his electric wheelchair and sits beside me as I study.

He's in his forties and has lost his speech because of his stroke. Despite the fact that I can speak and Paul can't, we enjoy each other's company. He stops me feeling lonely. I tell him all about my exam, all about my police work and all about the various points of law I'm studying. His face expresses interest and he laughs along with me. There's a railway station nearby. Every so often a train roars past and I can't be heard over the noise.

As much as I love learning again, it's a struggle. I can't underline sentences and take notes like I use to, because I've lost the power in my writing hand. I find that talking to Silent Paul, reciting the information I'm learning, helps me retain it. We make a brilliant pair.

When the Saturday of the exam dawns, I feel reasonably confident. I've studied for a month. I would never have had this much time to study if I was working.

As I drink a cup of coffee in the Forever House before travelling to the police college, I mention to Adrian and Diane that my neck is sore. It really worries me. Am I having another stroke?

'Maybe you slept awkwardly,' Adrian says.

'It's not that kind of pain.'

'What kind is it, then?'

'A pain like before my stroke.'

'Clodagh, I'm sure it's down to stress over the exam. Stop worrying.' Diane nods in agreement with Adrian.

We drive to the police college, but I don't feel reassured that the pain is exam nerves. When we arrive and I see student officers wandering around the grounds, I am filled with sadness. The last time I was here I was learning how to use a firearm. And this was the venue for my graduation, which was one of the best days of my life. And now here I am, with Adrian helping me transfer from his car into a wheelchair so that I can be wheeled around.

I feel self-conscious and put my head down, wishing I could cover it with a blanket.

'Adrian, please walk fast,' I say. He almost breaks into a run, and that makes me laugh. He pauses at a desk inside the entrance to the building. The officer acting as receptionist directs us to a small room, away from the main exam hall, so that I can shout out my answers to a police staff member without disturbing the other exam candidates.

Normally I hate being treated differently, but today I don't mind. I'm pleased, in fact. I really don't want anyone to see me here. Whilst most people can handle the fact I'm in a wheelchair, everyone visibly reacts when they hear my Chewbacca speech, which is still barely understandable. Their eyes fill with pity – and I hate that.

The police staff member introduces herself.

'I'm here to help you,' she says. 'Do you understand how this is going to work today?'

I nod. 'I say the answer I want and you mark it for me?'

'That's right. It's multiple choice.'

She takes my appearance in the wheelchair entirely in her stride, as if disabled officers appear every day. I'm grateful. The only thing is, the dull pain in my neck is still there. It's hard to concentrate on anything else.

The exam starts. I read questions about burglary, rape and other criminal offences, but all I can think about is the pain in my neck. I know it's not stress. It is something much worse. I think back to Easter-time, and the lead up to my stroke. I had a similar pain back then. Could I be having another brainstem stroke today?

I continue to point out answers, but I'm less and less sure that I'm getting them right. And I don't care. All I can think about is the pain in my neck. The doctors have told me that if I have another brainstem stroke I will die. Am I going to die today? And if so, why am I sitting here taking an exam? Why have I wasted a whole month studying, when I should have been spending every spare minute with my friends and family, enjoying life? These thoughts run through my mind on a loop.

I finish early. I know I haven't done well. I tell this to Adrian as he wheels me to the exit. Then someone shouts out my name. It's a friend and colleague, Flynn, who has taken the exam too.

I haven't seen Flynn since my stroke and he has a massive smile on his face. He leans towards me and gives me a tight hug.

'Are you still coming for a coffee?'

I want to say no, because I'm not feeling well, but I remember I arranged the coffee with Flynn earlier this week. I made the plan. I *have* to go. But by the time Adrian transfers me in and then out of the car, back into my wheelchair and into the café, I'm sure I'm having another brainstem stroke.

I try and act normally, but that's hard. Flynn presents me with a beautiful bunch of flowers and a coffee. He talks about work and the exam. He smiles, but all I can think is, *What am I doing here?* As we finish our coffee I say, 'I'm sorry, Flynn. Adrian, I'm having another stroke. I just know it.'

Adrian dismisses it again as stress and tries to reassure me. He reminds me that I'm taking medication to prevent another clot. But I tell him the pain is the same as before and that I want to go. We politely say our goodbyes and leave.

By the time Adrian has helped me transfer from the wheelchair to his car, I'm crying hysterically. I'm convinced that I'm having another stroke.

'It's okay, Clodagh,' says Adrian. RABIU is only ten minutes away.'

We arrive and he wheels me to my room, then goes to talk to the nurses. They run into my room and take my stats.

'Clodagh, you're fine,' they say. 'Everything is normal.'

But there's no convincing me.

'They said that the last time! They sent me home!' I sob, and Adrian hands me a tissue.

'I'll get a doctor, Clodagh,' says one of the nurses. She runs off and we wait, anxiously, for her return.

'I'm sorry,' she says, when she reappears, minutes later, sounding out of breath. 'He's unavailable right now – he's in another part of the unit.'

I lose my temper. 'I'm having a stroke and no one cares!'

Adrian looks at me, then glances at the nurses and shrugs, 'I'll take her to A & E at the Royal.'

'She just needs some reassurance,' they say.

He wheels me to the car, transfers me inside and drives at speed, but when we arrive at the Royal and report to A & E, they ask me to wait. I can't believe it. Why does no one ever believe me when I say I'm having a stroke? Not this time. If I wait, I'm going to be dead. I need to be checked out right *now*.

I begin to scream. Two nurses run to me and try to calm me down. But I'm like a wild animal out of control. They look at me with alarm.

'Just stay calm,' they say. 'Just until you can be triaged!'

I refuse to stop screaming. I know poor Adrian is bemused.

'What Clodagh is trying to tell you,' I hear him say, 'is that doctors have told her that if she has another stroke she will die. There's no time for triage.'

His words work. Within an hour I've had a scan. Then a neurologist comes to see me. Swishing the curtains to one side, he introduces himself with a slight German accent.

'You've been through quite a lot, young lady.' He examines my notes. 'But it's okay. You are not having a further stroke. The scan is clear.'

'What's wrong, then?' Adrian asks. 'Why is she in pain?'

'Where does it hurt?' he asks me, and I place my hand onto the side of my neck. He examines me carefully. 'You've pulled a muscle,' he says. 'That can be painful,' he adds. 'Are you overusing the less-affected side of your body?'

'Clodagh has been studying really hard recently,' says Adrian, explaining about the exam.

Looking at me, he says, 'I expect it was the way you were sitting while you were studying. But Clodagh, I understand why you were so distressed. Anyone would be in your situation. Do you feel reassured now?'

'No.' I know he's an expert – but I saw neurologists before my last stroke. They said I was fine, only that I shouldn't drive for 24 hours. And then I had a stroke. Why should this be different? Could he have missed something?

'You are only human. You might have made a mistake. Why not? Doctors make mistakes.'

'I see we're not convincing you. Would you like to spend a night on the stroke ward? Then we can keep you monitored.'

My instinct is to refuse. I have so many bad memories from the stroke ward – all those terrible sleepless nights. But I think about it and realise that, yes, it will reassure me.

When we arrive on the ward the nurses make a fuss of me, welcoming me like an old friend and marvelling at the improvement in my condition. I realise it's the right decision. I feel safe.

Adrian is still there when the night nurses begin their shift. He sees them before I do.

'I don't believe it!' he says and I hear him chuckle.

I turn and see the only two nurses on the ward that I didn't like, but it's okay. I don't mind. It's different now. I'm lying in bed, but I'm no longer trapped in my body. I can adjust my position. I can call for a nurse. I can speak up for myself. And, in the morning, I'm delighted when the deputy sister, Elizabeth, comes on duty.

'I've often thought of you, Clodagh,' she says. Her excitement at my progress is obvious. 'You've done so well.'

Elizabeth really cares about her patients. She oozes kindness. She asks me about RABIU and how I've managed the change.

'It was difficult for a while,' I say. 'I missed you all. I never thought I would!'

'Did you? You hated this place!' We both laugh.

'Yes – that was strange! But it was like starting again. Now that I'm settled, I really appreciate all the therapy.'

'That's good,' she says, looking thoughtful. 'Clodagh, I wonder ... could you do me a favour?'

'Me?' I'm surprised.

'We have a patient here, Paul, who is due to transfer to RABIU on Monday. He had a bad stroke too. Could you have a word with him and tell him what to expect?'

I nod, wondering if I am about to meet another patient who is locked in. But Paul, a man in his late fifties, can speak coherently. He's sitting up in a large, padded recliner when I'm wheeled into his room. He's a gentleman and clearly educated.

I tell him about RABIU, saying that, once you settle in, it's fine. I say I'll see him when he arrives. And that Monday, when Paul is wheeled into the unit, my life changes for the better.

He's there at dinner time and I introduce him to Silent Paul. We make general conversation and soon we discover interests in common. Like me, Paul loves to travel. I sit and listen, enthralled, as he tells me about his trip to New Zealand.

'You'd love it there, Clodagh,' he says. 'My wife adored it. She'd go back again in a heartbeat.'

I start to look forward to mealtimes again. Paul is a lecturer in engineering. He talks fondly about his students. I find him fascinating.

Siobhan notices a change in me during physio. She has noticed that, recently, I've lost enthusiasm for all my therapies. I tell her about the disaster of my exam morning and how worried I was about my neck.

'I was sure I was dying,' I say, 'and it was only a pulled muscle.'

'A pulled muscle doesn't feel like nothing,' she says, kindly. 'And with your right side being so weak, there's bound to be some added strain there.' She gives me new exercises to ease the strain and strengthen the muscle, so that it won't happen again.

'Clodagh, I notice your smile is back again. Have you met Paul?'

My smile gets broader.

'Yes. And I love him.'

She laughs. 'I knew you would!'

By the time Paul arrives I've been moved again. I still have my own room, but now I share a bathroom with the room next door. And, by happy coincidence, that's where Paul is put.

I've never enjoyed occupational therapy, mostly because of the constant attempts to get me cooking. I know it's a skill I need in order to regain my independence. But how can I enjoy it when it takes me a good ten minutes to open a packet with one hand?

In truth, I don't mind that. Everything takes me ages. What I really don't like is when the therapist tells me how to do something with one hand but never demonstrates it.

When Paul arrives, all that changes.

Now I want to cook. Now there's a point to it. I want to make breakfast for Paul and me. I get Adrian to bring in smoked salmon, because Paul likes it. I put it into our scrambled eggs and make it into a wrap. The nurses laugh when they see us heading for the O.T. kitchen together, in our electric wheelchairs.

'We'll have to tell Paul's wife about you,' they joke.

Paul has a wealth of knowledge about every subject we talk about – travel, stroke, food, even policing. He is full of obscure facts. He is able to understand me despite my breathlessness and the fact that I still don't speak very clearly. Paul is so positive about my recovery. I haven't met anyone else with his optimism about it.

I lend Paul my copy of *The Diving Bell and the Butterfly*, and afterwards we discuss it.

'It's beautiful,' I say, and he agrees.

Paul is like me – a voracious reader of books on stroke. He passes me one title, *A Stroke of Genius*, which I really enjoy. Soon we have an informal book club going. Occasionally, he reads car magazines too. When he's finished, he leaves them with me to pass on to Adrian.

I feel happy again, having found friendship with the two Pauls. I have breakfast with Lecture Paul and supper with Silent Paul. The wonderful thing about both men is that they listen to me talk. And I never stop talking.

Talking better has made such a difference to my life. My friends can understand me now and, when they visit, I make them take me out for coffee. I love talking. It doesn't bother me that I don't sound how I use to. Dinger, Fiona and Damien visit me regularly. I begin to let other work colleagues visit now I can talk. I love hearing all the work gossip.

It's fun. I enjoy being with them. The nurses tease me about how busy I always am.

One evening Dr McCann approaches me in the corridor. He pretends to be surprised to see me and says, 'Clodagh, I just wanted to check – you *are* still an inpatient here, aren't you?'

'Yes,' I say.

'Okay, good. But, Clodagh, you *are* aware that this is a hospital, not a hotel?' He smiles, to show that he's just being funny.

There aren't many patients who come and go the way I do. I'm beginning to feel like I have control again, that I'm getting my life back. From now on, I will live every day of my recovery to the full.

CHAPTER FIFTEEN

I Miss 'Me'

It's November. I've been home for two weeks. I dreamed of living here every day for the seven and a half months I was in hospital. It was all I wanted. Adrian and I spent a lot of time in rehab thinking about how it would be. We asked our families to stay away from us for a while, so that we could be alone together. They agreed. So it's been just Adrian and me.

Every day is the same. Adrian takes off the night splints I wear on my weak right arm and leg. Then he showers me – but it's not like showering and getting dressed in RABIU. Our shower hasn't been adapted yet and Adrian has to hold me on the now-mouldy stool we've placed in the shower as he washes my hair and body. I hate that I'm so reliant on him. I want to be able to do my own personal care. I can tell he is finding it exhausting, showering me every day, then carrying me to our bed afterwards so he can prop me up and dress me.

He annoys me when he pulls my trousers up too high and he always gets my socks wrong. It's irritating when the seam isn't in the correct place at my toes. On the leg I wear a day splint on, he pushes the shoe on with such force that I can tell he's fed up with helping me dress.

In RABIU I had teams of therapists and nurses to do these jobs for me. Now Adrian is doing it all himself. I think he's finally realising how needy I actually am, how demanding looking after me 24/7 is going to be. I'm like a newborn baby, except that I now talk back. I despise the situation I find myself in.

He cooks my favourite breakfast – poached eggs on toast, with coffee. The eggs are always perfect – soft, the way I like them. He gets it right every time. But we don't talk over breakfast – my speech is at its worst in the mornings – so Adrian sits eating breakfast silently. He looks like he has the weight of the world on his shoulders. We had fun during my weekends home from RABIU, but what used to be an adventure is now a chore. I rely on Adrian for everything. He hates it – I know he does. I hate it too.

I eat breakfast with a sense of dread in my stomach. I have nothing to do all day but sit in my wheelchair and watch television or read. I feel useless. Adrian will fill the dishwasher and empty it. He cleans up carefully but never exactly the way I like it. He leaves the dishcloth in the sink and lets teabags build up on the counter. Whenever I say anything about this he snaps at me. He makes the bed, does the laundry, cleans out the fire and lights the fire. He does it all. Every day. But he doesn't do it the way I like it to be done.

There is one thing he doesn't do – and that's help me with my exercises. I hate him for that. Adrian spent a whole physio session in RABIU learning from Siobhan so that he could help me. What a waste! I could have got my mum to learn instead. He says he's exhausted, that his life is all about the stroke now, that he needs 'me time'.

Without therapy I just sit all day in my electric wheelchair. Adrian won't let me do the exercises I used to do in the bathroom in RABIU. I fell dramatically in front of him once when I was trying. I smashed my face on the tiled floor in the kitchen where we used to dance. It was like a scene from a horror movie. There was blood covering the floor and blood covering my face. My mouth swelled up instantly and I cracked a tooth. I know it frightened him.

'Clodagh, you are worse than a child! You can't be left alone for two minutes,' he said as he cleaned my mouth and lifted me off the floor and back into the wheelchair. 'I can't keep an eye on you *and* do everything in the house. Just sit in that chair and stop trying to get out of it!'

Before the stroke I loved Adrian. And Adrian loved me. We never imagined that this would be in our future. We thought life together was going to be perfect. We used to enjoy spending time together. Now we hate being around each other. Have we been like hamsters on a rotating wheel – so busy dealing with the challenges of intensive care, the stroke ward and RABIU that we haven't stopped to think what we actually want? Does Adrian feel obliged to stay with me? Do we really even still love each other?

So much has changed since April, when the stroke happened. It was different when I was in RABIU. Evenings and weekends out with Adrian were fun. They were romantic, like dates. He had work and I had rehab. We had lots to say to each other and he enjoyed monitoring my progress.

Now we are back to everyday life, the realities of my disabilities have hit us like a ton of bricks. Adrian has taken leave from work to look after me but caring for me demands longer working hours than his job did. He complains that he's on duty 24 hours a day. This makes me angry.

'Do you think I want to be like this?' I shout at him. But when I hear my own voice it makes me sob. I'm sobbing every day now and it's eating away at his patience. One night he punches the wall in our bedroom, breaking the light switch with the force of it and cutting his hand.

I sob and scream at him: 'Just leave! Just get out!'

He reminds me every day that we aren't married and he doesn't have to be here. He has chosen to be with me and we'll get through this. But I tell him I want him to go. He tells me he knows I will beat this illness. But I'm not sure I believe him any more. I always thought I would – and I know he thought so too. But lately it feels like we have lost that belief.

Every night he drinks wine until we argue about me wanting him to leave. Every morning we eat our eggs in silence but forget about the argument the night before.

I want him to leave and be free, but I know I need him to stay. My mum and dad just won't cope if they have to look after me.

I was getting better in hospital. I was recovering. I could see it. And I had a team of people who were working with me towards that goal. I felt fortunate there. Some of the patients were unlikely ever to improve at all because the damage to their brain was so bad.

But now I'm home it hits me like a thunderbolt. I am not better. I can't look after myself. I can't walk; I can barely talk. This could be my life forever. I don't want to live my life like this.

I miss RABIU. I never thought I would say that, but I realise it's true. I miss the routine. I miss the nurses and therapists. I'm used to spending the whole day with them apart from the two hours of visiting time. They know how I like to do things. They encourage me to try to manage things on my own. They know I like to put on my own bra – with one hand and a clothes peg. They know I like to try and tie my shoelaces.

Adrian, on the other hand, can't bear to see me struggle.

'Why would you do that when I'm here?' he asks. He thinks he is helping but he isn't. I'm losing my independence. I'm losing myself.

The Clodagh Adrian started to date was really fit and healthy. She ran four miles every day. She was fun loving. She was in a demanding job that she enjoyed. Now she's stuck at home, helpless. Now he has to do every little thing for her.

I wake each morning and lie in bed, listening to Adrian breathe beside me. I think of the day ahead. A day that will be the same as the day before. The same boredom. The same frustration. I will never recover. I know that now.

The day I left hospital I was determined to walk out – and I did. But I had to hang on to Adrian for dear life and, really, it was only a few steps. I know I will never walk again – not properly. And I can't bear it. There's a dark cloud pressing down on me and I can't shake off the sadness.

Adrian does try every day to make life fun. When he goes to collect the laundry, he wheels me on the Stedy and hooks the laundry onto it. Then he wheels the Stedy into the utility room and puts the clothes into the machine. He *does* make me laugh, for a minute, but then, when he helps me back into the wheelchair and offers me a cup of tea, and I'm reminded that I can do nothing. Dark thoughts consume me and the heavy sadness I feel won't shift.

I used to think that where there is life, there is a solution. But now I realise there isn't. I have been consumed by this thought for two weeks. And no matter what Adrian does, or what television programmes I watch, or what I read, life feels meaningless.

I want to die.

We've had some work done at the Forever House recently. The bathroom has been converted for my use and the drive has been tarmacked to make it more accessible for me. We've taken money out of the credit union and Adrian has stashed it in the safe so that he can get it easily and pay the workmen. I've watched him carefully each day when someone has come for money and I've memorised the code. I've done that because he keeps the gun he uses for work secured there too.

For some days now I've been thinking about that gun, wondering if it's the answer. I don't want to live. Not like this. Not when it makes things so hard for all the people I love. I am no longer trapped in my body. It won't be easy – but if I use all the strength I have, I can end this torment.

One day I get my chance. Adrian says he is going out to buy some milk. I drive my wheelchair along the corridor from the kitchen to the room where the safe is. I carefully manoeuvre the wheelchair into the middle of the room.

I have to end this misery.

I punch in the code with my left hand. It takes a while. The safe swings open.

I sit and look up at the safe. Can I stand for long enough to open it? I try a few times, but fall backwards onto the wheelchair. This is impossible – I'm too weak. Then my eyes rest on my black stilettoes, bought just before I got sick. I wore them on a few nights out and was delighted that they were not just beautiful, but also comfortable to wear.

I can never wear those again, I think. *That life is gone.*

I have to end this misery.

Breathing hard, I haul myself to my feet. I sway and wobble as I get into the right position. Somehow, I manage not to fall. I punch in the code with my left hand. It takes a while. The safe swings open.

I get my hand around the gun and lift it out of the safe. I'm trembling madly. I guide the gun onto my knee. I drive the wheelchair into our bedroom, clutching it tightly. The gun is cold and heavy in my hand, yet it feels familiar.

I know how to use it. I've been using a handgun for eight years. Every day on duty I carried my gun to and from work just in case I came under attack from terrorists. Every day on duty I holstered it in my belt rig. I attended refresher training on the gun range two weeks before my stroke, making sure my skills and knowledge were up to date.

I know Adrian's gun is loaded and I know there is a round of ammunition in the chamber.

I notice Adrian's pyjamas carefully folded on the bed and I sob. But I have to do this for both of us, so that both of us can be free of this life. I wonder, briefly, who will miss me, but everyone I know has a full life. I am only a burden to them now, an object of pity.

Will Adrian be relieved? And then there's Diane, Mum and Dad. Will they despise me – or despise my memory?

I raise the gun to my head. I'm too weak to keep the gun raised, so I lower it and rest it on my knee. I wait until the strength comes back to my hand, then I raise it again. I'm ready. The gun is at my temple. My hand is shaking from the weight of it.

I hear Adrian's car coming up the drive. I have to do it now. But I can't. I sob, tears pouring down my face. A door slams and Adrian shouts, 'Clodagh, where are you?'

He appears in the doorway and his eyes widen in shock. Running towards me, he grabs the gun and throws it onto the bed.

'Are you serious? Are you serious, after everything?' He looks at me as if I'm a stranger. I can't meet his gaze. Tears blur my vision.

I've seen Adrian angry at work – but never like this. His face is red and I can hear the Belfast twang that only creeps into his voice when we're fighting.

He picks up the gun again and holds it out to me.

'Do it then!'

I look at him in shock. His eyes are bright. He holds the gun against my hand. 'Do it. Do it now, with me here, watching you. I want to be here to see you being so selfish as to end it.' He continues to shout at me, 'Do it! Do it! Go on! Now.'

'But you don't understand!' I scream.

'No, Clodagh, *you* don't understand. I've been here for you, always.'

'But you haven't lived it.'

'I *have* lived it.'

It is perhaps the first time we have been truly honest with each other. And the first time we've ever had an argument about *us*. We scream at each other. Then Adrian starts crying, and the two of us cry and cry.

'Clodagh,' he says eventually, crouching down to my level. 'You can't give up now. Not after everything!' He holds my head in his hands. 'We *can* do this. We *are* doing this. We *are* beating it!'

I feel selfish. So selfish. Most people who have locked-in syndrome would give anything to be where I am now.

'Let's go out,' says Adrian. 'You haven't been out in ages.' I realise he's right. In hospital, and when I was home for weekends, we always went out. But for two weeks now I haven't left the house.

We go to a supermarket together. Adrian hooks an adapted trolley onto the front of my wheelchair and pushes me around. We talk and even laugh as we go up and down the aisles, filling our trolley, and I feel the darkness that has consumed me slowly lifting. Adrian keeps kissing me on my head. I tell myself to stop being ungrateful and to start working hard again on my recovery.

When we get home he puts the items on my lap and I wheel my electric wheelchair around the kitchen, putting everything away in the right place. Coffee in the cupboard, bacon in the fridge. I feel useful.

'You see,' says Adrian, switching on the kettle. 'We're doing this. We're doing this together, and we *will* get there.'

Catching my look of doubt, he says, 'You know this isn't going to get better in two weeks. It will take years. But, Clodagh, we'll get there.'

We realise that we can't do everything by ourselves and accept that we need to let others in. We ask Mum to come every day to help me in the house. She becomes like a personal assistant to me. I know I can be difficult at times. I cry a lot. I cry when I get frustrated at the things I can't do. I cry when I cause damage to doors, walls and furniture with my wheelchair. I cry whenever the Paralympics are advertised on television because I'm jealous that I can't do any sport.

If Adrian hears me being difficult with my mum, he'll quietly tell me to be patient. She herself, I realise, has incredible patience. I develop a new admiration for her. She is stronger emotionally than I ever thought and the unconditional love she has for me amazes me.

But she struggles with my physical weakness, so Adrian gets me dressed – and that frustrates me. After the incident with the gun, he and I are too polite with one another. He keeps telling me to stop saying sorry.

Mum helps me to follow my rehabilitation programme. I instruct her in how to assist me with my stretching and movements. I continue to read all I can about stroke, learning about neuroplasticity and how to rewire a brain.

I learn how electrical stimulation can help stroke-affected muscles and where the electrodes should be placed on my body. I get my mum to help place the electrodes on the parts I can't reach. Mum and I enjoy this time together, while Adrian enjoys some freedom. Everyone benefits.

After Christmas Adrian returns to work, and it finally feels like I'm making progress. He comes home and tells me about his day, and I tell him about mine. I love it, and so does he. He drinks less now that he has returned to work, and we argue less. Mum starts to come earlier, helping me to shower and dress. As I get stronger, I can do more for myself.

I love online shopping. I never liked shopping before the stroke – I never had time with the hours I worked. But I find that online shopping allows me to be independent with some things. It allows me to get some control back in my life.

I buy my groceries online and get them delivered. I plan our meals, making sure they are healthy. I learn how to nourish my brain through food. I try to buy as much organic produce as I can. Feeding us good food gives me purpose. There are herbs growing on the windowsill now and the egg basket is always full. I tell Adrian I want to plant my own vegetables some day.

I begin to talk about the future again.

Eamon, the postman, interrupts me most days. One morning I hear the gate creak and, knowing that a parcel has arrived, I drive my wheelchair towards the front door.

Eamon hands over a package. He leaves and I open my latest purchase – a new recipe book. I'm binge-buying recipe books right now. I buy gadgets, too – anything that will help me to cook with one hand. Adrian tells me I'm a one-armed bandit.

'To think your signature dish, pre-stroke, was pasta with sauce in a jar!' he says as he tucks into my latest creation.

Mum is amazed at this change in me. She watches, amazed, as I crack eggs with one hand to make an omelette.

Adrian still has to do things for me. He still has to help me get to the bathroom, but now he walks in front of me, encouraging me to take steps, or sits in the wheelchair and drives it slowly, with me hanging onto the back and walking behind it. He makes it fun.

But the strain of living with stroke is starting to show again.

I'm focused on my recovery, and Adrian is working twelve-hour shifts and spending another two hours travelling to and from work. He's exhausted and, when we go to bed, he complains that he'll have to do it all again the next day. He's even started to complain about the time it takes to care for me. I can feel my anger towards Adrian starting to resurface.

When Eamon delivers an envelope from my aunt containing a voucher for a trip to a spa for Adrian and me, I'm delighted. I ring Adrian at once and tell him. He's enthusiastic.

'We need a night away, Clodagh.'

'But how will I manage with the wheelchair? Are wheelchairs even allowed in a spa?'

'There's nothing we can't do,' says Adrian, sounding happy. 'Just book it.'

He's right, I think, and I smile. It's a reminder of the Adrian I fell in love with. If we didn't love each other, why would we both battle for this? I book us in.

The day of the break arrives. I want to pinch myself. I'm actually going to a spa! I thought a spa break would never be possible again. Adrian wraps me in my white robe from the hotel, dons his own and wheels me over into the spa.

I worry that I will look out of place, but people don't react when they see me in the wheelchair. We chat, laugh and breathe in the smells. It is wonderful.

'Swim?' Adrian asks me. I say, 'Okay.' He has to carry me into the pool and hold me tight, because if he lets go I'll sink. It's wonderful feeling the water around my body, and Adrian's arms around me. I can't stop smiling. I stare into his eyes. They are full of happiness. I know he is reading the same thing in my eyes.

Afterwards we go back to the room to get ready for dinner. I wear a dress for the first time in ages.

'You look beautiful,' Adrian says, and I see love in his eyes.

I don't feel beautiful, but then Adrian hands me a black box.

The box contains a silver necklace with a single glistening diamond. I'm speechless – I wasn't expecting a gift. Adrian fastens it around my neck.

'Do you like it?'

'Of course I do! It's beautiful! Thank you!'

I look at Adrian and, as if reading my eyes, he says, 'We're better together, Clodagh. You're my wingman!'

We go down to the hotel restaurant, eat dinner and drink wine. I am happy and I know Adrian is too. We are reminded of how much we enjoy each other's company.

'We need to do more of this,' he says and I agree. We need to take lots of trips to get the fun back into our relationship.

'Adrian, I promise you – you won't have a lesser life with me.'

I'm more determined than ever to make that true. Adrian reaches across the table and squeezes my hand.

'I know that, Clodagh.'

Life is better now at home, but I have too much time to think. I look in the mirror every morning after my shower and don't recognise myself. Who is this person looking back at me? Clodagh *was* fit, with long, brown hair; *now* Clodagh has short hair, sits in a wheelchair and takes a cocktail of tablets.

Of course, everybody is happy that I didn't die, but in a sense the Clodagh I was before my stroke *did* die on that Easter Monday. I wonder if anyone else misses that Clodagh – the happy Clodagh who loved life, who loved to run. I know that I miss her.

I ask Adrian if he misses the old Clodagh.

'Yes,' he says, 'but the new Clodagh is nicer. She laughs more. You are allowed to grieve for the loss of the old Clodagh too, you know.'

'I don't want to say goodbye to the old Clodagh.'

Adrian tells me that what I'm feeling is a form of grief and that there are five stages of grieving. He describes the five stages. I identify with each one.

The first is denial. That was me in intensive care, when I couldn't believe I had suffered a stroke. The second, anger, came in the stroke ward, with my rage towards anyone who dared to cross me. Third is bargaining. Well, I did bargain with God. I told him if he just gave me back my speech, it wouldn't matter if I remained paralysed. Fourth is depression – and I almost killed myself.

'Stage five is acceptance. Clodagh. You have to accept that the stroke happened to you. You can't change it. Acceptance is not you giving up, it's choosing not to let your stroke beat you. It's building a new version of Clodagh Dunlop. And I think she will be even better.'

I think for a while about what Adrian has said. Was the old Clodagh truly happy? Not really. It's crazy. I had achieved so many things, but I always thought I wasn't good enough. I wasn't pretty enough; I wanted to run faster and be better at things. Adrian is right. I'm going to build a new Clodagh, who will be kinder to herself – who will like herself.

As Adrian and I sit in the hot tub, I think of all the times I feared I would never do this again. It's ironic – when we bought the hot tub, we didn't know how helpful it would be in easing the tightness in my muscles after the stroke.

We smile at each other and enjoy just lying in the warmth of the hot tub, looking at the stars in the night sky. Our favourite music is playing in the background.

Adrian looks thoughtful.

'Do you know the anniversary of your stroke is coming up?' he says.

I nod. 'A whole year – and I still can't dance. Or walk, come to that.'

'It doesn't matter. You're still here. How do you want to mark the first anniversary?'

I hadn't really thought about it.

'Dinner in our favourite restaurant?'

'No – you need something more dramatic to mark the day you nearly died,' says Adrian. 'What about a skydive?'

I laugh. 'That would be amazing!'

'And symbolic, too, since dreaming about it kept you alive.'

'But I probably won't be allowed.'

'You need a medical consent form. Well, we both do. But if we can get that, I know a skydiving company that will take us. I've already checked.'

He's right. Those dreams had kept me going throughout the times I could not move. And during those dreadful nights of overheating, before I had the spelling board, it was indeed the thought of the wind rushing as I dived that kept me alive. Adrian's right – it's the perfect way to mark the date.

We go to our GP. He signs Adrian's form but looks at me as if I have two heads.

'Clodagh,' he says, 'you have had a brainstem stroke. You can't possibly skydive.'

'My consultant says I'm medically fit.'

'Really?'

'I have mobility and speech problems, but apart from that I'm healthy.'

I give him my consultant's telephone number and luck is on my side. He gets straight through to her and I can tell from his side of the conversation that she's in favour of letting me skydive. But my GP's not for turning.

'I'm not signing, but I will fax the form to her and she will do it.' He shakes his head. 'Then you're her responsibility, not mine.'

As we leave, he is looking at me, shaking his head with incomprehension.

We book the skydive, but we don't tell anyone except Diane.

'How?' Diane says. 'After all you've been through?' Unlike me, Diane hates flying – it frightens her. But when she sees I am serious she hugs me and says, 'I love you, but you really are mad!'

When the day comes, Adrian asks, 'Are you nervous?'

'No,' I say. 'I can't wait.'

He looks puzzled. 'Do you remember last time? In Namibia? You were so scared when you were told to jump, you said, "I can't do this!" You screamed that at the top of your voice as they hurled you out of the plane.'

I do remember, and it makes me laugh. I think how bizarre it is that a moment I hated at the time kept me alive.

'Yes, but from the second the air hit me, I loved it!' I say, remembering how I fell through the heat, mesmerised by the scenery opening up below me.

As we walk out this time, it's cold, but my heart is so full of joy it might burst. Adrian holds my face and kisses me just before he lifts me aboard the little Cessna aircraft and positions my legs. The man I'm going to tandem skydive with sits behind me, already attached to me. Adrian sits opposite, grinning. It's just like the plane in Namibia – there's no door, just a gaping hole in the side to jump through – but we're not in Africa, we're in Northern Ireland. The weather couldn't be more different. It's so cold I can see my breath.

The plane rises from the runway and there is a green patchwork of fields below me. I could explode with happiness. I'm ten thousand feet above the ground and I'm not locked in any more. I feel truly alive and, perhaps for the first time since my stroke, I'm at peace. I finally accept what has happened to me.

I'm ready to jump. I sit at the edge of the gaping hole. My red suit is flapping furiously on my legs in the wind. I look at Adrian and mouth, 'I love you.' My tandem instructor tilts back my head and we fall from the plane.

It's exhilarating. My cheeks vibrate in the wind as we freefall through the sky. There is a sudden jolt upwards – the parachute has opened. I shout at the instructor to go slow. I want to savour every second of my descent.

In spite of the man strapped to my back, I feel alone again with God, but now I'm not arguing with him. Instead I'm saying thank you for all I have, and for the life I will have in the future.

I look across the sky and see Adrian hurtling down like a rocket. He turns like a corkscrew as he descends. As I come in to land I see him standing, looking up at me. As soon as I am firmly on the ground, Adrian runs over to me and gives me a hug so tight that I fear I might break. We grin and kiss. There is no need for words. We both know this moment should never have happened. I should still be locked in – dead, even. We've been to hell and back in this past year, but here we are now, together.

CHAPTER SIXTEEN

A Return to Duty

I'm ready to return to work.

It won't be to my previous uniformed role. I understand that. I have disabilities now. My dominant right arm doesn't work, I have to wear a splint on my right leg to allow me to walk and I use a walking stick. My speech slurs when I'm tired.

Occupational health and welfare have told me I'm on a 'phased return'. That means I won't return immediately to a standard full-time shift pattern. At first I will be on reduced hours; then I'll gradually build them up. I wanted to get back to full-time work straight away, but OHW explained that this was normal practice.

'Returning to work after a long illness can be daunting, Clodagh,' the OHW nurse said to me. 'A supported phased return can make the process easier. You do want your return to be successful, don't you?' I nodded. Maybe it was for the best. I didn't want to fail at this after working tirelessly all day every day on my rehabilitation to reach this point.

I'm determined to start driving again too, and I've passed an assessment with the DVA so that I can drive an adapted car. During the driving test I thought my brain just might explode. Mirror, signal, manoeuvre with one functional hand and what the instructor called a 'lollipop stick' felt like the most demanding task my brain had ever been asked to perform. But I did it.

Adrian and I travel to the garage to collect the new car I've picked out. It's been customised to allow me to drive with my left hand and left foot only. The adaptations can easily be removed to allow Adrian to drive it too. I feel nervous.

When the salesman helps me into the driver's seat and asks me what I think, I say, 'I love it.' Inwardly, though, I'm thinking, *Will I be able to drive this?* Adrian can read my thoughts and he says, 'Will I drive it home? Then I'll take you for some practice.'

'Yes, please,' I grin at Adrian.

I *do* love my new car. I'm excited about driving again. I hate having to depend on other people to ferry me around. It's just that driving feels a bit too complicated for my brain right now.

'You'll get used to the controls, Clodagh,' Adrian says as we leave the garage. I'm enjoying breathing in the new-car smell. He adds, 'Like everything, it's just going to take time.'

I'm a good driver – at least, I was before my stroke. I always enjoyed the times at work when I had to drive to an emergency and got to turn on the blue lights and sound the sirens. But driving the adapted car feels very different. Thirty miles an hour feels like ninety to me. It's not just because of my disabilities and because I'm driving with one hand. It's automatic, which I'm not used to, and the accelerator is where the clutch used to be. It's a whole new way of driving.

On Sunday, Mum and Dad come to visit. Mum insists I take the two of them for a drive in the new car. I'm apprehensive, but they persuade me to drive the short distance to Diane's house. Mum gets into the passenger seat beside me; Dad gets in behind me. Adrian gives me a kiss as we leave the house and whispers in my ear, 'Drive carefully.' We all put on our seatbelts and I drive up to the gate of the Forever House.

As we approach the gate to join the road we all see a car travelling in our direction.

'Watch that car!' Mum and Dad shout together in panic. I think clutch and brake. I put my foot on the clutch and it hits the floor. It's only when the car shoots across the road and crashes into the bank on the other side that I remember – what used to be the clutch is now the accelerator.

The airbags deploy. The car is filled with smoke. It smells like there's a fire burning inside it. For a short moment, the smell created by the airbag explosives makes me feel alive. But the continuous blaring of the car horn brings me back to reality.

I feel angry with myself. I'm such a fool. Opening the door, Dad asks me if I'm okay.

'Yes. Are you? I'm so sorry. I'm so, so stupid!'

'I'm fine, pet. As long as you're okay.'

We hear a moan from beside me. Mum is bent slightly forwards and looks like she's in pain. The colour has drained from her face.

'My chest is sore,' she says.

Adrian appears at a run. I can see worry etched onto his face. As he pats every part of my body, he asks me if I'm okay. I say, 'Yes. But look at my new car! It's a wreck. I can't believe I've crashed!'

'Don't worry about that,' he says, and tells us to go to the house while he takes the car off the road. Dad and Mum hold me up. My Bambi legs are even more wobbly than normal. Above us, lights flash in the evening darkness and the blaring of the horn follows us back to the house. As I reach the back door, the noise suddenly stops.

We sit in the kitchen in shock. Mum breaks the silence.

'I have to go to hospital. Something is broken.'

I suspect it's nothing serious – a bit of tenderness from the seatbelt restraining her, combined with shock from the force of the impact and the noise of it. But I agree that she should get checked out.

Adrian bursts through the back door.

'Clodagh, have you remembered that the *Belfast Telegraph* are due to phone to ask you about driving and returning to work?'

I begin to laugh.

'What am I going to say? I've just crashed the car and my mother needs to go to hospital? And I wanted to drive myself to work tomorrow on my first day back. I'll have to postpone!'

'No, you won't,' says Adrian. 'I'll drive you tomorrow. Tell them you can't wait to start back. Just don't mention that you've wrecked the car!'

Dad leaves with Mum to go to A & E, promising they will ring me with any news. Adrian makes coffee and, as he places a mug beside me, the phone rings. It's the reporter. We talk about work and, when she asks about my car, I say 'I love it. It's great to be back driving.' I don't lie – not exactly. I just omit to mention that my car is a complete wreck at the top of the driveway and that my mother is on her way to hospital with a possible broken sternum.

I'm anxious until Dad rings and confirms what I've suspected.

'It's bad bruising,' he says. 'She'll be sore for a week or so, but she's fine.'

I feel terrible but, knowing she is okay, I can breathe again.

It's Monday morning – my return to work – the day I have put in so much effort to reach. In the dream version, returning to work was not quite like this. Adrian drives me to my new station. I thought that when I returned to duty I would be driving, walking without an aid, talking more easily. It feels surreal. I don't object when he offers to walk me in. He opens the heavy blastproof door for me and follows me through.

I'm weak and wobbly and my right leg keeps going into spasm. I want to cry. Adrian touches my arm and says, 'You'll be fine. You can do this.'

I'm about to reply that I can't, but we've reached my temporary office.

There are men in uniform welcoming me. They smile and say hello, but I don't know them. I can tell they are men of a higher rank by the markings on their epaulettes. They are of a rank that only talks to someone of my rank when we're in trouble. We chat over tea. Everyone is nice, reassuring and welcoming, but my heart sinks. None of my old colleagues is here – not Fiona, not Damien, not Dinger. There's no one familiar at all. I'm back to the job I love, but it's not the same job. I'm no longer in uniform. I'm wearing civilian clothing and I have no idea what my new role is.

To my relief, Adrian has remained. We lock eyes as everyone talks. Since my stroke, we've perfected saying things with our eyes. Adrian's eyes are saying, *You can do this*; mine are screaming back, *I can't!* When the office empties, he kneels down to my level, places his hands on my thighs and says, 'Clodagh, change is part of life. This is a means to an end. It's *not* permanent.'

'I hate this,' I say. 'They don't know what to do with me.'

'Well, you can't go on patrol arresting people. You know that.'

I want to cry again.

'You will get a role you like in the end, but this suits you for now.'

I'm not convinced.

'Come on. You've been through worse than this! This is easy!' He smiles, and I agree reluctantly. Reminding me that he is always right, and that I was a good police officer and will be again, he kisses me and leaves. I sit alone in my new office, checking emails, and realise that during all the months when I have been working towards this I haven't thought about what it really means. Until now work has been my goal. Now I realise it's just the start of a new fight.

It takes me a while to settle in. For two weeks, while I wait for my new car to be ready, my parents drive me to work and home afterwards. It's like being back at school. Dad wants to walk me in, but I look at him fiercely.

'Don't dare get out of the car!' I say. 'I'm a police officer. I have to prove I'm fit to be here.'

It's hard for him. My illness has aged him. He didn't want me to join the police and he definitely didn't want me returning to work. He hates watching his daughter hobble in with a stick, and I hate it too. But I *have* to do it. I have to keep working; I have to get my life back. But right now I feel like a child going into kindergarten.

My job doesn't feel like police work. I am assisting other officers with the administration of their investigations in my old station. They are in a different station and working different shifts from me, so I rarely get to talk to them. Most days, that leaves me unsure of what's expected of me. It's really hard seeing people in the bottle-green uniform I used to wear. Whenever I catch sight of

Tactical Support Groups in their navy-blue boiler-suits, I have to hold back tears.

As I struggle to get my coat over my affected arm, a civilian staff member, standing in my office, using the photocopier, says, 'Home time, Clodagh?'

'Yes.'

She sighs. 'I wish I could have your hours.'

I want to shout at her, but I remain silent. Does she think that I *want* to be like this – unable to walk properly? Do they all think that? I'm supposed to be in the riot police, working 60 hours a week. I want that role so badly but I can't have it; and clearly she thinks I'm a waste of space. That hurts. The old Clodagh wouldn't have remained silent at this – she would quickly have given a smart reply.

But I accept my phased return. I realise that reduced hours means I have time to work on my recovery. I exercise in my home gym for two hours before work and two hours after work. When people mention my short hours I just laugh and say, 'Yeah, it's great! I'm heading home to relax.' This is temporary, I tell myself.

After Christmas, work gets slightly better. I get to review cases where people that are suspected of committing offences are wanted for arrest but police have been unable to locate them. Nonetheless, I miss my uniformed role. I miss responding to 999 calls but it's good to feel like I'm doing the job of a police officer. I tell myself to enjoy my phased return. Even though this role is one I don't particularly want, I should just be thankful I'm no longer a prisoner in my own body.

Every morning my mum helps me with exercises before work, straightening my twisted foot before putting on the bulky splint. One morning she asks me if I'm angry that this has happened to me. I laugh and tell her no. I have lived the alternative – I have been unable to move, unable to make a sound. I know that is how I should be even now. I understand, though, that *she* is angry.

I savour being able to move. It's exhilarating to be able to get out of bed, to feel carpet under my feet, to open my bedroom blinds and the window, to breathe in the outside air and to know it's the start of a new day. As I drive to work every day, I laugh, sing loudly and drink in the detail of the countryside around me.

I plan trips away. Adrian and I spread our wings. We take weekend breaks in European cities. I need assistance when we travel and, depending on where we're going, we sometimes bring my wheelchair. There's more planning involved than there was before, but we enjoy our trips more now because we're so grateful that we can take them at all.

When I stared at the pepper-spattered ceiling tiles in the Royal Victoria Hospital, unable to move, I would daydream about visiting Barcelona with Adrian. I would imagine sitting on Las Ramblas having tapas and wine, soaking up the sounds and smells in the summer sun as we watch the human statues startle other tourists with their sudden movements.

I'd imagine Adrian and myself dining outdoors on Plaça Reial under the night sky. When I'd get up to go to the bathroom someone might ask him how I'd hurt my leg. He'd just say, 'That's a long story' – because locked-in syndrome would be a fading memory.

I book a trip to Barcelona. We stay in a small hotel off Las Ramblas; at lunchtime the sun shines as we eat tapas there. We eat dinner on Plaça Reial. When I go to the bathroom the waiter does ask Adrian how I hurt my leg.

'Dreams are coming true,' he says, laughing, when I return to the table.

We are happy as we walk back to our hotel, our arms linked. When my right foot catches on a cobble, I fall, taking Adrian with me. Maybe because of the wine, maybe because we're feeling so carefree, we lie in an undignified heap, weak with laughter.

When we eventually pull ourselves together, though, I realise that my elbow hurts.

'I think I've broken it,' I tell Adrian – and we both start laughing again.

It turns out that I've only chipped it, though. So, undeterred, we plan more trips away.

My daily hours in the gym are paying off. I am getting physically stronger and my speech tires less. I'm sitting alone in the office one afternoon when I hear a voice I recognise.

'How are you getting on, Clodagh?' The voice is my superintendent. I look at him as he takes a seat. He's not in uniform, but he's wearing a suit with a bright red tie. He must have been at a meeting.

'There was a time when all I could do was stare at a ceiling – and that was more interesting. But I'm grateful to be able to work.'

He looks at me, then says, 'Would you consider a secondment to CID?' Officers are sometimes offered a temporary transfer to another position.

I jump at the chance. The trainee-investigators' exam, the one I took when I was in RABIU, has been advertised again and I've applied to resit it. If I pass, my temporary transfer could become permanent.

Within a few weeks the secondment has been approved. I feel nauseous as the detective inspector introduces me to the detectives in the team I'll be part of. He is wearing an oversized pinstripe suit and looks like he has been pulled straight from a TV crime drama. I warm to him as he explains the role of a detective within CID. I am to work alongside two officers, Tommy and Lee. I can't help but laugh – they look like stereotypical detectives from a crime drama too.

Within several months, on a spring Saturday morning, I sit the trainee-investigators' exam in my old station. I grin as I walk into the reception area of the building. I see colleagues I haven't seen since before my stroke. I talk and catch up with what is happening in their lives. Fiona bounces into our group – she's taking the exam too.

'Darling, are we still doing lunch after?'

'Absolutely!' We hug and wish each other good luck in the exam.

I have been practising writing with my left hand but, as much as my writing has improved, it is still not good enough to mark the exam paper by myself. As before, I am taken to a separate room and a police staff member marks the answers I call out.

This time I know the answers. When I finish, I hurry to meet Fiona for an exam debrief – and some gossip.

I drive us to lunch.

'Can you imagine us as detectives, darling?' giggles Fiona.

'I know! I just hope we pass.'

A month later, the news is good. We've both passed.

Since starting in CID, I've wanted to feel like I deserve my place in the team. Now I do.

Tommy and I have instantly hit it off. I tease him by calling him Thomas, which he hates. In return he calls me by my surname.

'Are you ready, Dunlop?' he asks.

'Yes.'

Tommy shakes his head and, smiling, says, 'What's funny now?'

'I'm happy to be going to court again.'

'That's good for us – then you can go every time!' says Lee, piping up from behind his computer.

Tommy is beside me as we walk into the courtroom. I've never been in this particular court before, but the layout of the room is familiar to me.

Tommy and I are dressed for the occasion. He has on smart trousers with a shirt and tie. I'm wearing my best navy trousers and a white shirt. I have bought myself a brown leather briefcase for the paperwork I need. It is slung over my shoulder. Am I beginning to look like a detective in a crime drama too?

We sit at the back of the courtroom.

'Are you okay?' whispers Tommy.

'All rise,' booms a voice from the front of the court.

Everyone in the courtroom stands as the judge walks in. When he sits, everyone else sits.

My stomach flutters. I don't know when I'm going to be called to give evidence. Can I do this? I thought I could. I hear sounds but I'm not really listening. I feel a nudge to my arm. Tommy is looking at me.

'You're first.'

I feel conscious that everyone in the court is watching me as I walk the short distance to the witness box. My heart thuds. I move slowly and deliberately, gripping my walking aid and praying the entire way: *Please don't let me trip.*

I make it safely into the box. A court clerk hands me a bible. Standing, I hold the bible in my left hand and say the oath, 'I swear by Almighty God that I will tell the truth …'

'Detective, put the bible in your right hand,' booms the Judge.

I turn my head away from the microphone in front of me and lower my voice. 'I can't. I have right-sided weakness.'

'The detective cannot. Carry on.'

Tommy and I laugh about what happened as we drive back to the office. I feel relieved that not putting the bible in my right hand was the only problem I had in court. My first time back has been successful.

Tommy takes me out to incidents to instruct me in the skills of being a detective, and Lee keeps me right in the office with the legislative parts of my role. I feel like a proper police officer again. Tommy and Lee don't make me feel that I'm less able because I have disabilities. I get a left-handed mouse and a tablet to record statements. I even write with my left hand when I know the statement won't be more than a few pages. My handwriting is improving. There is always some way to overcome the problems I encounter. The only thing I can't seem to overcome – for now – is walking without an aid.

I work hard in the gym at home, and at the gym at work. I know it will help my walking in the end, but I wish it would happen faster.

A new detective called Lisa starts in the office. I instantly like her – she feels like someone I've known all my life.

'Why is there a Chewbacca beside your desk, Clodagh?' she asks as I'm putting on my coat. We're due to go on a house search together.

'It is to remind me, if I'm having a bad day, that there was a time when I'd have given anything to be where I am now.' I will never forget shouting 'Ahhhhhh!' in RABIU and Lesley calling me Chewbacca.

I stand in front of ten uniformed officers, to whom I am to deliver a briefing about the search. Lisa takes a seat beside them. I explain the specifics of the search. It's the first time I've briefed anyone, and it will be my first house search, since I've been back.

You don't know how momentous this is for me, I want to tell them. I catch sight of one of my old colleagues. She spoon-fed me smoothies in RABIU. It's surreal to be standing briefing her and her team. I look away quickly, worried that if I don't I will cry.

I finish and we all drive to the search address.

'Pass me my stick, Lisa.'

'I don't think you need it, missy,' says Lisa.

'I do.'

'I'll be beside you. I know you can do it.' Lisa says this to me in such a way that I believe her. I leave my walking aid in the car.

I never use it again.

I can walk but I can't run – yet. I decide to buy a recumbent trike so that I can do the next best thing and go for a cycle. That way I can be out on the roads again at least. I tell Adrian, 'It will keep me happy until I can run again.'

He has reservations.

'It's very expensive – the price of a small car, Clodagh,' he says. 'Will you be able to pedal it? Your right leg is still weak.'

I am not put off. In fact, Adrian's doubt spurs me on. I find someone in Devon to supply the trike and fly it over to Belfast, where it will be adapted to suit me – with all the gears and the brake on the left-hand side. I wait, impatiently, for the trike to be ready.

The day comes. I drive to Belfast with my mum. When I sit on the trike for the first time, I can't stop smiling! Mum smiles as I cycle around the forecourt of the shop. I love to see her smile. The worried look she had permanently on her face has disappeared. I'm shown how to fold it and, having placed it in the boot, I drive home. I can't wait to show Adrian that I can now exercise outdoors again – and I'm proud to have managed the entire project myself.

Adrian comes out to meet me as I park.

'Let's see this bike that cost as much a car,' he says sarcastically. Making his way to the boot, he starts to lift out the trike. I stop him.

'I can do this myself. I *want* to do it myself.' I lift the trike out of the boot with one arm. I catch Adrian's and Mum's eyes. I know they are having to stop themselves from helping. Unfolding it, ready for use, I feel like I did when I was a child, when I got a new bicycle at Christmas. 'Let's go for a cycle now.'

Adrian agrees and we change into our running clothes. Pulling on my running tights after all this time feels like a dream. I want to pinch myself. 'Let's do our old four-mile running route,' I say.

'Do you think you can?' Adrian doesn't sound convinced.

We leave together on our bikes; my heart is so full of happiness. I can't stop laughing and Adrian is laughing just as loud. There are green hedges on either side of me; the wind is in my face.

We reach a long downhill stretch.

'I'm alive!' I scream, loving the sense of speed and sheer exhilaration. Adrian shouts behind me: 'We've got out lives back!'

And so we have. Life is different, yet its essence is the same. It is simply more beautiful now. I enjoy every second of every day, knowing that in the blink of an eye life can change. This is my second chance. I am blessed to have had 35 years of being able bodied and carefree. Part of me feels guilty that I have lived through locked-in syndrome and come out the other side. I will never forget the times when I was a prisoner in my own body, completely helpless. Now I appreciate what it means to live and to love. Now I see the beauty in every small part of my life.

I appreciate my family and friends more now than I did before illness. I appreciate the incredible individuals who work in our health service. I have shared my recovery publicly on Facebook and I'm grateful to each of the 7,000 people who have liked my page and followed my journey. I recognise that without the kindness and love, patience and positivity of everyone with whom I have had contact throughout my illness, I wouldn't be where I am today. I can never thank each person enough.

And, for my part, I will never give up. I will be the best that I can be – whatever that is!

People tell me my recovery is a miracle. Maybe it is. But I believe this for everyone: if you work hard for whatever you want – if you never give up – you just might find you create your own miracle.